Poet
of the
Revolution

Poet of the Revolution

The Memoirs and Poems of Lal Singh Dil

Translated from the Punjabi

by Nirupama Dutt

PENGUIN
VIKING

An imprint of Penguin Random House

VIKING

USA | Canada | UK | Ireland | Australia
New Zealand | India | South Africa | China | Singapore

Viking is part of the Penguin Random House group of companies
whose addresses can be found at global.penguinrandomhouse.com

Published by Penguin Random House India Pvt. Ltd
4th Floor, Capital Tower 1, MG Road,
Gurugram 122 002, Haryana, India

Penguin
Random House
India

First published in Punjabi as *Dastaan* by Chetana Prakashan, Ludhiana 1998
First published in Viking by Penguin Books India 2012

Translation copyright © Nirupama Dutt 2012
Photographs courtesy Parnab Mukherjee (page x), Diwan Manna (pages xlviii, 126)
and Swaranjit Salvi (page 160)

All rights reserved

10 9 8 7 6 5 4 3 2

ISBN 9780670086559

Typeset in Garamond by R. Ajith Kumar, New Delhi
Printed at Replika Press Pvt. Ltd, India

www.penguin.co.in

MIX
Paper from
responsible sources
FSC® C016779

This is a legitimate digitally printed version of the book and therefore might not
have certain extra finishing on the cover.

Your Time

When
a million suns die
then
your time will come.
Isn't it so?

Lal Singh Dil

Contents

Foreword

Pages Saved from the Storm

The first difficulty that I encounter in writing about Lal Singh Dil is the fact that I am not good at remembering dates and Dil never wrote dates on his letters.

I think it was the summer of 1971 or 1972. By then a large number of Naxalites had either been killed or captured by the police. Surjit Hans was here from England. I went to meet him in his Sarabha Nagar home in Ludhiana. Amarjit Chandan brought Lal Singh Dil to see us there. Dil with his short stature and dark, round face held no attraction for me. But I was impressed by his poetry. Chandan had given me Dil's diary and I had published five of his poems in *Lakeer*.

In the evening, we sat on the terrace, drinking tea and trying to talk. However, the conversation was not really flowing. Chandan and Dil went away. Surjit Hans had to leave for Delhi early next morning. I caught the bus to Jalandhar because that very day the police had raided the Sarabha Nagar house. Dil had been brutally tortured by the police after the action at Chamkaur Sahib. He had served three horrendous years in prison and he looked scared.

After some time I read a letter from Dil. It was written from some obscure place in Uttar Pradesh in which he mentioned how he was walking by the railway line with thorns digging into his feet when, in the cold moonlit night, he passed through a jungle and saw the crescent moon etched on his palm. He was singing the tarana of Faiz, *Badhate bhi chalo, katate bhi chalo*. This spiritual experience resulted in his being drawn towards Islam. This letter brilliantly conveys the thoughts and feelings of a militant poet losing his mental balance. I regard it as a unique achievement in Punjabi literary prose. The incident described in the letter forms part of Dil's memoirs.

When Lal Singh Dil embraced Islam—first becoming Muhammad Bushra, then Wali Muhammad and then Wali Muhammad Samralwavi—and wrote his first Urdu verse in praise of the poet Rasool before penning ghazals, his restless body and soul found peace. It is evident from his letters that he has found shelter in a great power.

In a letter from Mohammadi, he writes: 'Yes, I am telling the truth. The leather workers wash their face with water from the same lota used by those who write the Quran and those who spread the religious word.' He was trying to say that the Brahmin and the Chamar were using water from the same utensil. This was something that put his troubled mind to rest.

I received one letter from Lakhimpur Kheri. It was evident from his letters, many of which are lost, that sometimes he worked with the imam in the mosque, sometimes he was caretaker of the factory, sometimes he looked after the orchards, sometimes he became a cloth vendor moving from village to village. He also lived in a timber godown. He became a cook for the landlord, worked as domestic help in the home of a thanedar and was a farm help for three Punjabi brothers.

During this period he put together a manuscript of his poetry. It was dedicated to the Jungli Buddhist. I was amazed at reading his poems. When did he find the time to write such wonderful poems? Amarjit Chandan took the manuscript from me and published them under the title *Bahut Saare Suraj* (A Million Suns). I think he wrote these poems while working at the farm. His mental health was fine and he was inspired to write these poems after reading Pandit Jawaharlal Nehru's *Discovery of India*, as he says in one of his letters.

He returned to Samrala in 1982. My wife's nephews had supported him at the mosque. One day, on a visit to Samrala, I ran into him. Dil was wearing chequered pyjamas and kurta, a worn-out brown woollen waistcoat and a matching prayer cap. He had shaved off his moustache and his eyes were lined with surma. Looking at him, I was reminded of many working-class Muslims. True enough, Dil had lived among Muslims in Uttar Pradesh, who were not miserable in their poverty but considered themselves blessed because they sat with the Pathans, Mughals and Turks in the mosque and performed namaz with these kindered folk whom they called brothers.

Dil spoke humbly with downcast eyes. He spoke as though he were a representative of Islam. He told me he performed his namaz five times a day. He did not take any intoxicant. He was also preaching Islam and converting people to this religion. First of all he had made his mother recite the Kalma and become a Muslim because Jannat lay at a mother's feet. If he had not converted his mother, the doors of heaven would had been shut to him forever.

Hearing him talk like this, I was reminded of his old letter which he had written soon after converting to Islam. He had written that the name of Mao should be erased from his writings because the name was sinful. He had also said that whatever he had written in praise of God should be burnt.

Who was this Lalu? Many images were overlapping in my mind. There was no anger or rebellion in Lalu. He seemed to be a sadhu or saint. His speech had traces of the Uttar Pradesh accent. He was also using Urdu and Arabic words.

He told me that he still had one desire and that was to get a burqa stitched and marry a Muslim woman in Malerkotla. He did not care even if she were a widow. Hazrat Mohammad Sahib too had married a widow and this was a very holy thing to do.

We travelled by bus from Samrala to Khanna. From there we started walking to my village Badgujran. Throughout the three and a half miles he kept talking about himself, and how he was blessed in his new role as a Muslim. He said he had received a lot of love from the Muslim brotherhood.

Whenever I asked him if he had found a woman's love, he would avoid the topic or confess that wherever he lived he sought out an unmarried woman and kept looking at her or thinking about her. He would imagine that one day he would marry her. One fascination would end and another would begin, and this would go on but Lalu was never disappointed. A nikah was not for him and, not surprisingly, it never happened. But Lalu was satisfied with his fantasies.

Once he came back from Uttar Pradesh to Samrala and forced his mother to get him a burqa made for the woman he was going to marry. His mother sold the wheat in the house and raised money for the burqa. As a result, it became difficult for her to survive. Later a time came when Lal's younger brother would call his mother home for meals but not Lal. The mother would eat some of the food and hide some rotis in her chunni and bring them for her son.

There was a time when Lal had no work at all. He would sit with the baba in the cremation ground. The baba would share his meal with Lal and his dog. Lal would talk to the baba and intake poppy husk. He had also learnt to meditate. He would sit for long hours, meditating on Amrita Pritam. After Nirupama started taking him from his tea shop for beer and cigarettes on the bridge over the Neelon, he would keep wondering what she would eat and where she would sleep if she moved in with him. He also meditated for long about a woman leader. Once he found a white marble in the cremation ground. He wrapped it in a silk handkerchief and told everyone that it was a naagmani. If he came across anyone ailing or unhappy, he would read the Kalma and touch the person with the marble to drive away the demons.

Lal has not written about any love affair with a woman in his memoirs, he has only given indications of his fantasies. He even talks in abstractions. Comrades accuse him of several things but I am sure he has never seen a woman unclothed. When Chandan was here, Sukhwant Dhadda was shooting a film on Lal. I interviewed Lal and he admitted that there was no woman in his life.

When he is sober, his eyes are downcast and he talks softly. When he is drunk his eyes shine and he shouts out his words. He stares but never complains. He does not want to labour any longer to earn his bread, nor is he capable of hard work.

For a couple of years he was the imam of the Samrala mosque. He would lead the namaz on Fridays but another maulvi would take away the offerings made by the devotees. He started working at his friend's tea shop because both of them would sit together and drink tea.

When I heard that he had opened a tea shop in partnership with Lal Din of Malerkotla, I was happy. But when I went to meet him there I realized the shop was not able to pay even the rent. The painter Surjit Kaur gave him Rs 2000 and stocked up the shop. But after three months it was empty once more. Then Lal set up a tea shack with a friend. I asked him, 'How much do you earn?' His reply was, 'Enough for the liquor at night.'

Drinking in the evenings started when Master Sarod Sudeep started holding literary meetings at his home in Samrala. Gulzar Mohammad Goria would also be there. Once Sarod had a fight with one of his neighbours and he invited Lal home every evening to scare the neighbour by saying Lal was a terrorist. After sunset, Lal would say yawning, 'Master, send for some liquor. I have even finished my bundle of bidis.'

Various groups started honouring him after Nirupama began to write about him in the *Indian Express* and his book *Naaglok* (City of Snakes) came out. As soon as the award money came into his hands he would take on the role of the bold militant. Now he has patented this role.

He wrote his memoirs at our behest, when his mental condition had somewhat recovered. But there is still a certain incoherence in his writing. Unfortunately, many pages of his writings were lost in a dust storm. We recovered some pages but some were lost forever. Then an MPhil student borrowed the manuscript and sat over it for a long time. However, one benefit was that he made Lal write many of the lost pages all over again. We have edited this manuscript several times but the incoherence remains, manifested in a feverish intensity that we wish to retain. We are sure that the readers will find this work memorable as it is. It is not just an autobiography. It is a testament to Dil's unforgettable prose and great poetic vision.

28 July 1998   Prem Prakash

Introduction

Always a Lover, Always a Poet

From a tea vendor to a revolutionary, from a daily-wage worker to a mullah in the mosque, Lal Singh Dil has assumed many roles in his life. But through it all he was a lover, a poet and a madman, all in one.

Translating the memoirs of Dil and his poetry for this book has meant knowing Dil anew, going deep into each word, each image, trying to resurrect in English the life, times and poetry of one of the finest poets that the Punjabi language has known. This has been an intense experience which has had its moments of great highs and sometimes unthinkable lows. That is perhaps the lot of most writers and more so of Dil who was ever struggling to strike a balance between his immense poetic talent and the harsh reality of his life.

My introduction to his name and poetry happened way back in the 1970s when another prominent Punjabi poet, Amarjit Chandan, asked me to translate two of Dil's short poems for an anthology of Naxalite poetry that was being published in Kolkata under the title

Spring Thunder. I reverently did so. In those days the left
had its literary and intellectual aura. But when I tried to
make inquiries about the poet, I met with a deadlock.
He was hailed as a major Punjabi poet of the Naxalite
movement. Then he seemed to have disappeared from
the scene altogether: gone underground, moved to
Uttar Pradesh and converted to Islam. For many in
the literary circles, he had become an obscure figure.
He had served his purpose and no one talked about
him any more. I too forgot all about him. That was a
decade when poetry flourished and there were many
poets around, so it did not quite matter if one called
Dil had vanished as quickly as the spring thunder.

Nor did one come to know of his return from
the orchards in Uttar Pradesh to his hometown in
Samrala—which was the birthplace of another wild
child of literature, the Urdu fiction writer Saadat Hasan
Manto. It was not till the early 1990s that I met Dil and
that too by chance at a poetry symposium organized
by Jalandhar Doordarshan.

He was nothing like what I had expected. Dil was
a frail man in a kurta-pyjama and a woollen khadi
jacket. He wore a turban with one end loose, Bhagat
Singh style, and said little. But there was something
irresistible about his smile. It went straight to the heart.
Even in his frailty, he had an enduring presence and I
felt somewhat proud that I was reciting my poem from
the same stage as Dil. I had come from Chandigarh in a
cab and I offered Dil and his poet friend Sarod Sudeep a

lift back to Samrala, for it would mean spending some more time with the legendary poet who had become a kind of phantom figure. The two accepted my offer and went on to buy a couple of bottles of beer for the journey home. My drinking days were not yet done but I was a rum guzzler. Anyway I swigged a few gulps from Dil's bottle in the general bonhomie. What touched me most was that Dil, while buying his bundle of bidis, had taken care to buy two loose cigarettes for me.

This was not all. As the diesel-fed old, white Ambassador cab puffed its way from Jalandhar to Ludhiana, I felt Dil dig his elbow into my side and ask me—in soft-spoken English, if you please—'How old are you?'

He had not learnt that one should never ask a woman her age, and perhaps he was a bit disappointed because the honest woman's reply was, 'Almost forty.'

He was quick to say, 'But you don't look it. You look hardly twenty-eight or twenty-nine.'

He had won my heart for all time. Here was a man who was all gallantry and charm. A few months before Dil got his freedom from life, we had organized a small event at Chandigarh in which young Parnab Mukherjee gave a theatrical performance entwining a story of Mahashweta Devi with the poems of Dil. I was to talk about Dil and as I recounted the 'twenty-eight, twenty-nine' remark to tease him a little, he was quick to reply, 'You still look twenty-eight or twenty-nine to me.'

Ah! Dil, I believe you. It is interesting to see the male

interpretation of Dil's platonic attention to women.
His friend and mentor Amarjit Chandan writes:

> Lal never got the companionship of a woman, so his
> portrayal of the pain of womanhood is imagined and
> removed from life. Whatever we yearn for, whatever
> will never be ours, becomes an ideal. Lal considers
> woman to be an ideal as vast as earth itself. Woman is
> always mysterious even with her travails, but even the
> destiny of man is not without its pain. This feeling is
> always present in Lal's poetry. The pain becomes a part
> of his being.

Others were not so kind and mocked the crushes he
had, which ranged from the college girl with two plaits
to Indira Gandhi, from the likes of me to the celebrated
Amrita Pritam. In fact, for someone like me, who has
not experienced the 'companionship' of a man, these
flights of fancy seem quite in order.

When I first met Dil, who had been the subject of a
number of MPhil and PhD theses, he was selling tea in
a shack opposite the motor market of the Machhiwara
road in Samrala. The comrades of his revolutionary
days were now editors, executives, professors,
businessmen or expatriates. The spring thunder was
over and everyone had returned to the comfort zone
of their class structures. Dil had his kachcha home in
the run-down Kang Mohalla or Chamarian, as some
referred to it. He was at a loose end and did not know

what to do. His parents had aged and his brothers were trying to make ends meet, doing small jobs. It was then that Chandan, who had been the first to publish Dil's collections of poetry—*Satluj di Hava* (The Satluj Breeze) and *Bahut Saare Suraj* (A Million Suns)—had gathered money from friends in England and sent it to Prem Prakash. Dil's hovel was then remade with brick and mortar and he was asked to keep busy writing his autobiography. His father passed away and then his mother. Now there was no one left to see that Dil got a few morsels of food every day. He needed a livelihood and so a tea shack was opened for him by well-wishers.

My acquaintance with Dil begins where his memoirs end. Eager to go back to Samrala, I suggested to my editor in the newspaper a story on this rare poet who was working as a tea vendor. He happily gave me the go-ahead and there I was in Samrala. Turning right from the bazaar on to the Machhiwara road, I started my hunt for the tea shop. Twice I must have passed it and twice I missed it. Then some local boys led me right to the shop where I found Dil with a cloth tied around his head. There were several people having tea there including an educated middle-class gentleman in a wheelchair. Newspapers were scattered around the shop and the bench and there was Dil with his partner, a tall Sikh man called Pala, a misfit in his upper-caste Khatri Sikh community because he smoked. Later I was to learn that he was an opium addict who was trying to rehabilitate himself. And so it all started over a cup of tea.

The shack was made of planks of wood nailed together. It had a kerosene stove, a dented kettle, a dozen cheap glasses and a meshed-wire tote. The tote could hold six glasses and was used for delivering tea to the motor market folks. There was also a notebook for keeping accounts in which Dil scribbled couplets, for he was still in the 'ghazal' mode. He had brought this notebook with him from Uttar Pradesh. But his fame always rested on his blank verse and it still does.

The mission to interview and photograph Dil was not so easy. Since I did not have a camera and there was no photographer accompanying me, I told Dil to wait as I went to arrange a photographer from a local studio. When I returned to the tea shack, there were a few other people but no Dil. He appeared for a few seconds only to disappear again to bring a few more people. So finally there were twenty to thirty people he had assembled there including mechanics, drivers and others. Dil told me, 'I never get myself photographed alone.' 'We' remained important to Dil all his life and I was reminded of an instance in his memoirs when he tells his tormentor, a deputy superintendent of police (DSP) named Pannu, that he never drank tea alone. So it was a group photograph, with my little daughter and I becoming a part of it and Dil there as a speck in the crowd.

Explaining the importance of friends, he said, 'Do

you know why King Dushyanta did not recognize his love Shakuntala when she came to him? Because she was alone. When he had first met her she was among her friends. Similarly, I will not be recognized if I am alone.'

Coming from anyone else, this may have sounded affected, but not Dil for he always spoke from his heart—*dil se*—whether he was talking to his tormentor DSP Pannu or a new admirer called Nirupama. After the group photograph was done, I was able to get a few photographs clicked of Dil and Pala in the act of tea-making.

An interview amidst the throng of Dil's comrades seemed difficult, so I suggested that we go to the nearby Neelon tourist resort which had a lovely view of the canal. So Sarod Sudeep, Dil, my daughter and I started for Neelon. I was keen to drink some beer with Dil, although I hate beer. We ordered beer and pakoras and sat on the grassy slope by the canal. This second meeting with a few swigs of beer was to be recounted as a 'scandalous' encounter or some great turning point in Dil's behaviour many times by Prem Prakash, editor of the Punjabi literary magazine *Lakeer* and a friend of Dil's.

Dil was carrying a diary with him in which he had prepared some notes for me. 'It would be wrong of me to talk of myself straightaway before talking about the two great poets of our times,' he said, and started off on a long treatise on Mohan Singh and Amrita Pritam.

Now, I knew my Mohan Singh and Amrita Pritam well. It was Dil I wanted to know better but knowing Dil required time and patience.

Sure of his own poetic merit, he was still shy of talking about his poetry. But after a bottle of beer down his throat—which must have been very little, used as he was to much more and much stronger country liquor—he did start talking about his life. He rambled on, moving from one thing to another. First he told me that he had once challenged the police not to implicate him in an opium case because that was too petty in Dil's grandiose scheme of things. 'So they charged me in a revolver case instead,' he said with pride. Then he recalled that special plant that grew in the plains of Uttar Pradesh where he had gone in exile. After that he switched topics again, dropping his voice to almost a whisper, and said, 'You know when I was arrested, Chairman Mao came on Radio Beijing to announce the news and say that Dil was very dear to him.'

I did not blink an eye as he said this; and then he added, 'I do not know if Queen Elizabeth made the announcement on the BBC or not.'

This was Dil living on the edge of delusion and reality, swinging from Chairman Mao to Queen Elizabeth and leaving the listener quite speechless. And he did all this with a poet's flourish.

Samrala soon became a favourite stop whenever I was travelling through Punjab. Once Dil saw me outside his tea shack and started scolding me, 'You must inform

me and come. You just land up without any notice.'
I was a little taken aback. He explained that he
required time to gather gifts for me. 'People forget
many things in buses and I was hoping to find a
cigarette lighter for you. This time all I have for you
is a small notebook.'

Those days Dil was getting truck drivers to write
lines of poetry instead of jokes and abuses on the back
of their vehicles. 'Why must they write "blacken your
face" and other such rubbish? I want to replace it with
a line or two of good poetry.' One line which I can
recall is *koonjan udd jaana* (the birds will fly away).
Incidentally, his last gift to me a few months before he
died was his own cigarette holder: 'I wanted to buy you
a cigarette holder but the shop at Samrala was shut for
some reason. So I am giving you my own.' The little
polished-wood holder with a brass tip meets my eye
every time I open my trinket box.

The news feature on Dil which was printed in the
Indian Express caused quite a stir. Dil was popular
enough in Punjabi but this was the first time his story
was revealed to the readers of English: 'Naxalbari bard
sells tea for a living.' A few days after the story was
published, the editor called me, asking for Dil's address.
Apparently, the chairman of the Punjab Scheduled
Castes Land Development and Finance Corporation
wanted to help him by giving him a loan to start a dhaba
and earn some money. I gave the location of Dil's shop
and the necessary contacts.

I did not know the outcome until I decided to make yet another trip to Samrala. This time my mother and daughter were with me and we were to stay with Sudeep and his family. Dil too reached there and I asked him if he had been offered a loan.

'Yes, they wanted to give me a loan of one lakh rupees. Now, I am a poet, and who knows when I may die. Then they would talk ill of me saying I took their money and died,' said Dil, half-joking, half-serious.

It so happened that the corporation kept pressing the loan on him, reducing the amount each time so that it would not be difficult for him to repay the instalments. However, it was a point-blank no from Dil every time. Finally he accepted a grant of Rs 5000 from them and so it was party time for Dil and his friends in Samrala for the next couple of months.

That evening Dil took me round the town he was so proud of. We went to Pala's home and met his beautiful wife and daughters. En route he told me, 'Pala's eldest daughter was married off to an elderly man because Pala owed him money. Now, isn't this exploitation?' It was with great pride that he showed me his new pukka room and then he made a generous offer: 'You come and live here. Write what you want. No one will trouble you here.'

Through all the ups and downs of those turbulent years, I felt secure in the knowledge that there was Dil's room to retreat to. Then he shared with me a grievance against his brother's wife. 'You know what she has been saying? She says I do not have any family and my home too will go to them. She is illiterate and does not know what she is saying but it hurts me.' Ours was what the famous Urdu poet Faiz Ahmad Faiz described long ago as *dard ka rishta* (bond of pain) in one of his couplets:

Badha hai dard ka rishta,
yeh dil ghareeb sahi;
tumhare naam par aayenge
ghamgusaar chale.

The bond of pain is strong
even if the heart be impoverished;
those who share your sorrows
will be there when you beckon.

However, I could do little for this bond of pain but write about him and occasionally, when we met, share a bidi or cigarette and listen to Dil talk.

Some years later, carrying a copy of the *Little Magazine* in which I had translated an extract from the story 'Memoirs of a Tea Vendor' with a photograph of Pala and Dil making tea, I reached Samrala and found Dil at the cremation ground. Pala's last rites were being performed. Long after everyone else had left, we sat there side by side by Pala's flaming pyre. Dil kept talking softly as tears flowed down his cheeks.

The years that followed were not easy. Dil no longer

ran his tea shop. He had closed it down some two years ago when Pala had fallen ill. When I next visited Samrala, I started looking for Dil at the spot where the tea shop once stood. It was no longer there. Whenever in Samrala, a search had to be made for Dil. Each time I have found him at a different spot—the mango grove, the tractor repair shop, the cremation ground or the liquor shop—everywhere but home. This time Dil was in the home of the Hakim Sahib, who had just shifted from Old Delhi to Samrala. It was Eid so we were treated to red-hot chicken curry, rotis and phirni made by his wife who, Hakim Sahib proudly said, was a Punjabi from Malerkotla.

The next day inside Dil's home in the Chamar basti, images that stood out were of the few wooden planks of the tea shop, stacked up perhaps for firewood, and two flower beds that he had built on his kachcha kotha (terrace). A few roses were in bloom. Every now and then his little grandniece would come crawling up the stairs, asking her uncle for a toffee. No matter how harsh life might have been, there was still room in it for a few green leaves, a flower or two, a child's smile and some sweetness.

—◦—

Before I start indulging myself by going further down the winding by-lanes of my memories of Dil, it is more important to see Dil in the context of Punjabi literature and his position as a Dalit writer. Dil's literary status in the world of Punjabi literature was never disputed, and the celebrated Punjabi poet Surjit Patar says, 'He will be counted as one of the major Punjabi poets of the twentieth century.'

It is pertinent here to quote from an article by Dr Harbhajan Singh, a well-known poet and scholar, on his first encounter with Dil's poetry:

Lal Singh Dil has sent me a copy of his poetry anthology, *Bahut Saare Suraj*. On it he has written: 'To Dr. Harbhajan with love.' By coincidence it has reached me when people are busy sending one another New Year cards. The book is printed on cheap newsprint and at places the ink is faint and at other places there are blotches of excessive ink. From the front cover to the back cover there is nothing that will attract a reader to open it. I do not feel like opening the book but how could I ignore this New Year gift. I follow my instinct and open the book at random. These are the first lines that I come across:

> The fragrance of cheap and old clothes
> extending to cheap soap and cream
> No greater joy comes their way after this

There is nothing in the essence of these lines that can be called alluring but still they are able to pierce my heart deeply. These lines bring to the mind the wedding of some poor girl. A poor girl is always married off in old and cheap clothes. She is made up with cheap soap and cream. In the vast sea of sorrow that she has to traverse all her life this is the only fragrant island. I feel that these lines are very close to me and some compulsion had separated me from them. That same unconscious compulsion makes me turn the pages to get rid of these lines and this is what I see next in this book of cheap fragrance:

> If the inhabitants of other planets
> would learn of this
> they would turn to stone
> and never rise again
> If animals were to
> experience this
> they would run to the forest
> screaming in fear of humanity . . .

A shiver runs through the soul. This message printed on cheap paper is very valuable. These lines written in bitter truth put me to shame. First, I feel ashamed that why I have started expecting that good poetry should be written on good paper and printed well. When we are describing dusty lives then even the packaging can be dusty. I feel I belong to some other planet and have turned into stone. I no longer feel the pain of the other. Lal Singh Dil's lines hit me hard. Lal Singh Dil is a truly new signature in contemporary poetry.

Amarjit Chandan, in an assessment of the poet after the latter passed away, writes:

His name epitomizes his personal history—Singh (lit. lion) is an acquired middle name from Sikh culture and Dil (lit. heart) is a nom de plume after the Farsi romantic poetic tradition. Even the acquired names could not give him any social identity. In reality he was Lalu—a Dalit who suffered all his life at the hands of a caste-ridden society, the Communist Party and the state structure. After disillusionment with the idea of instant revolution, he self-exiled to the UP in the early 1970s where he worked as a cowherd, a house servant, a watchman and a peddler. He converted to Islam changing his name to Muhammad Bushra and saw Mao and the Prophet Muhammad as saviours of humanity though he did not write any poem about the latter.

It is said that time is a great healer. What Brecht wrote is as meaningful: 'When the wound stops hurting, what hurts is the scar.'

Dil is a unique poet in the sense that his work is experiential and meets all the literary standards. His poems stand out with their subdued tone and simplicity. In them one can see the scar of his wound inflicted by social exclusion and unrequited love. His poems run like a silent, slow-motion film with stark imagery of the wretched of the earth. A single line from one of his poems sums up his aesthetics: 'Scared, the birds / start singing all of a sudden.' He was such a being who could sing against all odds.

———

There was much to Dil's life that is difficult to slot. It was a life of immense struggle but celebration too in the purely Punjabi style. His story bears witness to the deep-rooted, inhuman discrimination in the name of caste. Although a creation of the Hindu way of life, it is found in all major religions that are based on reform or conversion from Hinduism. Sadly enough, it has also been a part of the left cadres, which ideologically do not recognize religion, caste or creed. So Dil's various attempts to transcend the caste barrier by joining the Naxalite movement of the late sixties in Punjab or later converting to Islam with the new name of Muhammad Bushra met with frustration that his simple poetic heart rebelled against.

Punjab has a higher of percentage Dalit population than other states. Scheduled Castes form about 30 per cent of the total population and 8 per cent of these castes live in the rural areas and are landless. The landowners are mostly Sikh Jats. The Dalits follow the religion of their masters as per old practice.

Born to a low-caste Ramdasia Chamar (tanner) family, Dil was the first of his clan to pass tenth standard, while doing his daily labour, and go to college. He was training to be a schoolteacher when

Naxalbari intervened. Dil's poetry was true to his life and that of those around him, and the experience of poverty, injustice and oppression was so real and told so well that he was hailed as the bard of the Naxalite movement in Punjab. In his dream of a society free of caste and class, Dil saw a new dawn for the oppressed.

However, the extreme left cadres were not untouched by caste prejudice, and when the movement was crushed the torture meted out to the Dalits by the upper-caste police was far worse. Dil went underground and moved to Muzaffar Nagar in Uttar Pradesh. As a caretaker of a mango orchard there, he came in contact with Muslim culture. Once again, he saw the possibility of escape from caste oppression and converted to Islam. In a long letter written to Chandan, he revealed his decision, saying a crescent moon had appeared on the palm of his hand, and added a line: 'Allah is very kind to Maoists because he understands cultures.'

Interestingly, the red haze of the times did not allow Chandan to feel the intense emotions contained in this letter or the experience of transformation that the poet was undergoing. He published it in *Hem Jyoti*, an ultra-left Punjabi magazine of those times, with the comment 'Lal Singh Dil is Dead' for he had accepted religion. Later, Chandan was to regret this epithet and acknowledge embarrassment for being so judgemental. He also expressed the hope that Dil in his largesse would have forgiven him. And so Dil had.

The undated letter that was written in 1973 was later described by Chandan as a 'great piece of Punjabi prose'. It is reproduced in full here:

Bismillah Rehman-e-Rahim.

Dear brother and brothers, Salaam-Alaikum.

I received your letter and read it several times. Let me first tell you that I have become a Musalman. This happened a year ago. I have been circumcised, I have learnt to perform the namaz and I have also gathered the required knowledge about the religion. This has not happened by chance. Even earlier my heart craved for Islam whereas my head had been gifted to communism. I was an atheist so the heart too was given to communism.

One winter night I was treading the dangerous path in the jungle all alone. That night I was under the spell of many movements, many faiths and many songs: *Katate bhi chalo, badhate bhi chalo . . . Allah hi Allah ho . . . Allah hi Allah ho . . . Kajara lagake, bindiya sajake . . .* I was singing these songs with such abandon that even my own heart was contracting in fear. Even if I sing so now, it has the same results. At times that night I would turn into Babur astride a horse, and at times I would become the horse. Other times I would turn myself into the changed landscape of China's culture, become the fearless Ranjha or turn myself into a stork flying all alone to Madina. Here I come, I would sing to the tune of a flute. I was carrying some colour powders in my shoulder bag, some roasted potatoes, one knife, some toys for children that were poking my side and there was a doll that whistled on being pressed. I was also carrying a copy of the *Lakeer* magazine with my poems published in it, a [packet of] hair remover and wounds of the circumcision. That day well before sunset, I had seen the crescent moon engraved on the palm of my left hand. Only an artist could have carved out such a beautiful miniature moon. Some flesh had been carved out of the hand and I had coloured both my hands. I kissed the moon over and over again. The moon is still there on my hand. Whenever I see it, I kiss it and say, 'Allah is Supreme.' After that I burnt all my possessions, removed every hair from my body and consigned to the flames my non-Islamic clothes. Now I wear a tehmat with a kurta, a jacket and a white namaz cap. I shave off the hair from my head, trim my moustaches and wear my beard four fingers long in the Arabic cut. I perform my namaz nine or ten times during the day and night. All this has happened by the grace of Allah. I have not been able to write anything so that is why I did not send a letter for so long. However, I have not been able to distance myself from what I have written so far. This is so because I have read in Qalam Paak that Allah says that he will create such a community that will be a sword for the infidels but compassionate to the believers.

May Allah forgive me if I am wrong, but the community that he was referring to is the one of Maoists because the political waves are moving in this direction. So my sympathies are with the community of Mao and

Ho Chi Minh because they are a part of Allah Tallah's politics. The cultural waves excite me but I am a follower of Allah Saleh Muhammad Mustaffah. Thus I seek pardon from Allah Tallah for my loud sloganistic poems in which I said I have turned myself into the father of God. Forgive me Allah!

I learn that you have come out of jail. Congratulations! I had sent a hundred and ten poems of which I no longer have a copy. If you are going through those poems to prepare a manuscript . . . Please dedicate my book to Allah Saleh Chand Muhammad of Madina. It is a sin to photograph ourselves in Islam. Write back as soon as you get this letter.

My name: Muhammad Bushra,
Muhammad Bushra Chowkidar,
Janta Oil Mill, Mohammadi,
District Kheri (UP)

—◆—

Dil's conversion to Islam was yet another way of trying to change not just his world but the world around him. And he hoped to find a wife for himself in his new faith. But marriage was not to be for him, so Dil returned home to Samrala in 1990, after Punjab's long night of terror ended.

For five years Dil said the morning and evening azan. Alone and addicted to cheap liquor, he became the caretaker at the mosque with Gulzar Mohammad

Goria, who sent him two meals a day from his home. Born in Saadat Hasan Manto's birthplace—Papraudi village—in 1955, the year Manto died, Goria was a Punjabi teacher in a government school and a left-of-the-road short fiction writer. A CPM activist and a constant friend to Dil, Goria died of cardiac arrest two years after the poet's death. Goria recalled, 'God is everywhere but our effort in opening the mosque was directed at giving confidence to a minority community that should not be afraid of going to its own place of prayer. However, when people started coming to the mosque, the Wakf Board intervened and took over and now Dil and I are persona non grata there.'

Well, the Wakf Board must have had its own reasons because, political ideology apart, Dil and Goria were a bit too fond of their drink. Thus it becomes impossible for poets and writers to play clerics. The great Ghalib has said:

Zahid sharaab peene de masjid mein baithkar,
Ya wo jagah bata de jahan par Khuda na ho.

Priest, let me sit and drink inside the mosque,
Else tell me that place where God cannot be found.

Years later Dil told me, 'Caste prejudice exists among the Muslims too.' This was a scathing comment on how the 'Manu-made' evil had percolated to every other religion and 'ism'. However, Dil remained a devout

Muslim performing namaz, keeping roza (fasting) and eating only halal meat. While he did not put his last wish—to be buried—on paper, he had articulated it to his close friends and relatives. Goria told me, 'The wish was communicated to his brothers and left-wing activists. However, there was no Muslim burial ground in Samrala as the Wakf Board had leased out the ground to a sadhu, who had built a temple there.' It would have meant taking his body to the neighbouring village of Bhaundli but it may not have been accepted there so Dil's brothers conferred and, even though they respected the fact that he had converted to Islam, they decided to cremate him in the Dalit cremation ground as they had done with other elders of the family. Goria added, 'We did not wish to rake up a controversy that would make Dil the Muslim overshadow Dil the great poet.' Much was denied to him in life, and even after death the system could not fulfil his last wish.

A great poet he undoubtedly was and his collections of poetry, *Satluj di Hava* (1971), *Bahut Saare Suraj* (1982) and *Naaglok* (City of Snakes; 1997), as well as his memoirs, *Dastaan* (1998), enjoy an exalted place in Punjabi letters. His long poem of over a hundred pages—which builds a case for the wretched of the earth, including labourers, marginal farmers, school and college dropouts, addicts and the oppressed women of Punjab—was published some two years after his death. It has been acclaimed as one of his brilliant works, written when he was battling with disease, addiction and deprivation that had always been his lot. The book is called *Billa Aj Phir Aaya* (Billa Visited Again Today; 2009). Talking about this book, which was supposed to fetch one lakh rupees from the publisher—he died before getting the money—Dil mocked a senior Punjabi novelist, Jaswant Singh Kanwal, saying, 'Kanwal has not been doing his job as a novelist. There is no mention of the vanquished youth of Punjab today: the addicts and the victims of suicide. So even though it is not my job, I have had to write a novel in verse.'

The memoirs open with a very young Dil going to school. The alphabet primer in Urdu has a sign that reminds him of the spindle he sees in the blacksmith's shop on his way to school. Unable to comprehend the words of the morning prayer uttered at the morning assembly, he would think the students were saying, 'Roorh, the blacksmith, makes spindles . . . Roorh, the blacksmith, makes spindles . . .' This was Dil's own little prayer or perhaps his first poem before he actually started writing poetry. The joy of school is lost when Dil realizes that he belongs to the 'other' group—the untouchables.

As the poet recalls his childhood, we are brought face-to-face with a sensitive boy who is curious, frightened and sometimes indignant at the world he sees around him. The writer in him appears even before he goes to school when he encounters a book for the first time in his uncle's cupboard. His uncle reading out the legend of Nar Sultan to his friends in the evening is something Dil remembers with a thrill. The fantasies and fears are narrated so vividly that the reader relates to them, becoming a child all over again. Inside the shy and quiet boy burns a fiery furnace as his mind questions the indignities heaped upon him. In all innocence he joins boys bathing by the well only to be thrashed, for he has entered the sacred arena of the upper caste. The next day Dil's mother has to go and apologize to the mother of the boy who thrashed him instead of the other way round.

An amalgam of such big and small experiences makes the young Dil suspicious of the goings-on around him. There is confusion and anger and as an adolescent he gives a blow on the head to a picture of Mahatma Gandhi with his cowherd stick as he passes a signboard in the bazaar, where he has gone chasing a runaway cow. Beneath the picture was written that just as a pitcher of milk was ruined by a single drop of poison, a society was ruined by the malaise of untouchability. It took him a long time to realize his error for he had mistakenly read 'untouchability' as 'untouchables'.

Come youth and the poet's heart is aflutter. He is attracted to a few girls but proximity comes with a dimpled girl and the two steal a kiss. Yet the sweetness of it is soured when Dil visits her home and her mother throws the tumbler from which Dil has drank tea into the fire to purify it as they belong to an upper caste.

Dil's memoirs are not merely confessional and cathartic but offer deep insights into the poet's mind and the world around him. A wry humour laces the entire narrative, even when he is talking about his mental breakdowns. That was Dil for you, a man all sincere and honest. His purity and innocence made him a great misfit in a world full of guile. Solace comes to him in the form of bidis or cigarettes and later liquor.

The episode at the Chamkaur Sahib police station has a Kafkaesque streak to it because Dil is tormented and tried for a revolver that never was in his possession. When the policemen are torturing him to get information, they tell him that they know him well and that they have heard him recite poems at different symposia. At this Dil wryly comments that all that these 'uniformed' fans of his poetry could give him were beatings and torture.

Dalit Naxalites had it bad—both from their party and from the state. The underlying caste anger is reflected in the refrain of the tormentors: 'So you bloody Chamars, you want our land?' In spite of it all, the zest to live and create remains with Dil.

Dil was a wayward legend in his lifetime and now his poetry lives on, as does his struggle and protest. He had told me that one day people would come and sing qawwalis under the banyan tree outside his hovel. It will happen one day, for in 'Manto-town' Dil was the true fakir and Manto and Dil are forever embedded in many a heart.

Personally for me Dil remained a source of strength. I felt that if Dil could survive thus there was no reason I could not. The fight and the song were always his almost to the very end and I took much of his strength and energy to battle my own demons. Let those who would like to call it a mutually reciprocated crush between two romantic 'outcasts' do so. Well, there are outcasts and there are outcastes. As far as romanticism goes, pundits of the West proclaimed that it would succeed postmodernism. Ahead of our times, weren't we?

When news came of Dil being taken ill and then hospitalized in Ludhiana, I had joined a new job and had to go to Delhi for work. I reassured myself saying that Dil would pull through. In fact, Parnab, after a visit to Samrala, had said in a long poem, 'Lal Singh Dil is a stubborn man.' Indeed, he was stubborn to have lasted sixty-four long years in spite of everything. I was halfway to Delhi when I learnt that he was no more.

I went to the large condolence meeting held outside his house in Kang Mohalla. People from all walks of life were there, writers, poets, theatre activists, drivers and mechanics of the motor market, Muslims and Hindus, his family and of course the leaders of the left, from the tame CPI to the fiery Marxist-Leninists. Willy-nilly, Dil was an icon who could not be ignored and more so after his death. It was ironical that many of left leaders, all from the upper castes, who had taken every possible benefit from the state, were suddenly screaming, 'Dil was ours, he is ours and he will always remain so.'

This, when the pension of a 100-odd rupees from the State Languages Department meant for old and ailing writers had never reached Dil's home. I once mentioned the pension and Dil cried out, 'I don't want this pension from the state. I am a poet of the Naxalbari.' I was glad that the dole never reached him. He lived with pride and died with pride.

The last ten years of Dil's life saw him get various honours, which included some cash awards, given by small left-wing and Dalit literary groups. His room was full of trophies gathering dust; many of them bore the picture of Bhagat Singh. Having become a Muslim, he said by way of apology, 'I do not believe in putting pictures on the wall. It is not part of my faith. But these have been given to me with love so I keep them.'

Over the lunch that followed the speeches to mark his passing, a friend of Dil's told me, 'In the hospital, a day before he passed away, he said he wanted to face the side where he could see the nurses come and go.' Didn't I say he was always a lover and always a poet until his very last breath?

I was reminded of Dil telling me about his favourite film of 1960 vintage—*Dil Apna Aur Preet Parai*. Many may not recall the film but it had some wonderful music and one of its numbers, '*Ajeeb dastaan hai yeh*', continues to be an all-time hit. The film told the heart-wrenching story of the thwarted love of an orphan nurse for a surgeon. The surgeon is obliged to marry the spoilt daughter of a rich man who had financed his medical education. I saw the film on video some twenty years after it was first released and it touched a tender chord. For Dil it was the last film he saw: 'I saw the film at Minerva Theatre and then saw it a dozen more times because I liked it so much. After that I never saw any other film.' Was Dil searching for the lost orphan nurse, played by Meena Kumari in her heyday, among the nurses in the hospital?

When Dil passed away and the news reached Chandan in London, he wrote me a line on email with the biblical reference, 'Free at last!' Yes, Dil had got his freedom from human bondage. We all like to honour the memory of those we have cherished. Watching Dil grow frail over the years, I told myself that one day soon we shall learn that the slightly crazed man who sells tea and writes poetry to be painted on trucks, performs his namaz in the mosque and heretically drinks country brew is no more.

Dil was given no burial and no mazaar was built in his memory. But his poetry will forever linger in many hearts and minds. A poet's story is never complete without his poetry, so these memoirs also have a section of his selected verse. Each chapter also opens with a few lines from his poems and this act of translating and editing has been for me no less an honour than placing red roses on his tomb which—like the house without walls and windows (*bay dar-o-deevar*) that Mirza Ghalib envisioned—has no structure but still exists.

Nirupama Dutt

MEMOIRS

Fiery Furnace of Childhood

Words have been uttered
long before us
and long after;
chop off every tongue
if you can
but the words
have been uttered.

There was a time when I was trying to write about
what had not happened in my life. In other words, I
wanted to negate the events I had experienced to see
what course my life would have followed without
them. Now, however, I am at peace with all that has
happened because poets have to cross the river of fire—
in my case, the flaming red Satluj—to keep the little
lamp in their hearts ever ablaze. This little flame goes a
long way in sustaining them on the path to creativity.
I have endured the ordeal by fire time and again in
my lifetime, and it is a miracle that I have been able
to emerge unscathed. Once, for instance, following a

Brahmin who resembled Tagore, I entered the little pool of water by the well where the Jat boys were bathing. I must have then been in either class II or III. I was wearing a dirty shirt and torn drawers. The water drawn from the well was flowing in a torrent from a spout and I had just crouched down to put my head under the water when a Jat boy pulled me out and gave me a thrashing. Nothing happened to him, of course. Instead, my mother had to apologize to his mother for my dreadful mistake of entering the sacred space of the upper caste. She admonished me and told me never to go there again. By narrating this incident, I'm not trying to establish that the powers that be had wanted me to be beaten thus; nor do I want to credit it to fate. What I am trying to say is that this experience was essential to my understanding of the world around me.

My conscious memories of school begin when I was in class I. I recall a vivid image from that time—a collection of sparkling white uniforms. The legs of the table in front of me and the chair I sat on are engraved in my memory and somewhere, that chair is very important. I was four years old and Chacha had taken me along with him to school. I do not remember how we went to school or returned home. A book was lying open in front of me. On one side of the page there was a column of single letters. Later, I realized that it was an Urdu primer. On the other side of the page there were small words; and between the letters and the words was a sign which looked just like the blacksmith Roorh's takla or spindle. I remember it so well that I can still draw it out on a sheet of paper. This spindle was etched in my mind for many years. When the children would say the morning prayer at school, I could not fathom the words and would imagine that they were saying over and over again, 'Roorh the blacksmith makes spindles . . . Roorh the blacksmith makes spindles . . .'

Roorh's shop was on my way to school, and I must have seen the spindle there. So when I came across the sign in the Urdu primer I was immediately reminded of it. However, I did not go to this Urdu school for long. I was born in 1943, and by the time the country was partitioned in 1947 things had changed considerably. Many Muslims were brutally killed in the violent upheavals of the time, and those who survived fled to Pakistan. Afterwards, all Urdu schools in our part of Punjab were shut down.

There is another story from my childhood which connected me to the spindle.

My dadi, who had been widowed at a very young age, used to share all the sorrows of her life with me. She had three children—my father, a blind daughter and a younger son. However, her younger son fell off a cart and died in the hospital. My grandfather was resting on the terrace when the terrible news reached him. The shock was too much for him to bear and he died at once. His body had to be suspended on ropes and brought down. My father, my grandmother and her blind daughter were the only ones left in the family.

But the sorrows did not end there. My blind aunt, who was married in a faraway village, was shattered when she received the news of her father's and younger brother's deaths. The poor woman was so disturbed that she started hammering her stomach with her fists. Her liver got damaged and she died a few days later.

Dadi used to tell me that my father worked for the zamindar, looking after his cattle in return for a few rotis a day. Dadi would make some money by grinding wheat for one paisa a day. She would save that paisa and, on returning home, would dust the flour from her clothes and make a roti for herself. She had learnt to live with hunger. She also told me that my mother once threw her out of the house. Not just that—she even hit her hard when the older woman was spinning yarn and broke her spindle. Thus, the takla is closely linked with my childhood memories.

❦

Never have I thought, even in my weakest of moments, that I should have been born in a happier or more affluent environment than was my lot. I had seen even those boys who came from upper castes and affluent homes being ill-treated by callous teachers. Sometimes, I would even go to their homes.

There is one incident of my childhood that I remember very well. Once my mother took me to her parental village holding my hand and making me walk all the way from Samrala. I was tired and wanted her to carry me. As we were crossing the Jhumluti village field, we heard a voice calling out to us. I turned around and saw a man grazing his cattle near a grove of trees. As I stared at him, he turned away. It was much later that I understood the whole episode. He was singing a line from a folk song: *Mera digea rumal pharhavin* (Pick up my handkerchief and give it to me). He was obviously flirting with my mother. She got scared and held on tightly to my hand. We started running. On reaching a small garden that had a well, we quenched our thirst. There was a 'Sadhu Baba' in the garden who inquired about my mother's welfare. The rest of the journey was uneventful.

My mother would stop every now and then to talk to passers-by. We had neared Ghug village, which had a dominant Muslim population. Many children gathered to greet us and carry me home. The children called me a town boy or shehari. My mother had two brothers and there were several cousins who were now carrying me around fondly. My older uncle was always busy tanning leather at home. I would go and disturb him. He would smoke a hookah and straighten out pieces of leather. I would examine my uncle's treasures with great interest. I recall walking around the room, looking at the things that were kept in a cupboard embedded in the wall and attempting to lay a hand on the array of sharp instruments and screws there. He would poke the horn of a deer in my nose and scare me, saying, 'The jackal is coming!' The base of his hookah had two claws that, to my mind, resembled the feet of a jackal. I was familiar with the howling of jackals even though I had not seen them. But from their howling I imagined that they would be something like dogs. He had another mischievous ruse up his sleeve—he would surreptitiously tickle my ear and say, 'Here comes a rat!' This was his way of playing with me.

My uncle's son Jailla was my age and together we would go through my uncle's tin trunk and the cupboard. The topmost drawer of the cupboard had incense sticks and other such material. The second drawer was full of his tools—sharp iron instruments like chisels, hammer, scrapers and knives. The bottom drawer was stacked with wooden frames and other waste. We could never find a jackal or a rat. Jailla found some books and these included the legend of Nar Sultan. There was another thick book that I could not understand. It was a book on Ayurvedic medicine and after my uncle's death one of his sons-in-law took it away.

My mother's younger brother used to work as a siri, or landless labourer, for the landlords. This amounted to becoming a slave, whereas the elder one did his own leather trade and thus had more freedom and dignity. The former was quite a character. He would roam about with a stick in hand even though he was practically as thin as the stick.

One evening a strange thing happened—something

that distressed the whole family and also the neighbours. People were peeping out of their hovels to see what had happened outside. At the end of the street was a well from where everyone fetched water. A woman was returning home with a full pitcher when her husband started beating her on the street and broke her pitcher. Enraged, my uncle picked up his stick and went out looking for the nasty man. The neighbours brought my uncle back home and advised him not to entangle himself in the husband–wife scuffle. But he was livid and said, 'Why did he have to break the pitcher outside our house on a Thursday? It is an ill omen.'

My uncle had come home late from work that night. He kept chatting with my mother for a long time. My mother was so busy with her relatives that I started feeling very lonely. I wanted to run back home to Samrala. A round ventilator was cut into the wall and I could see the glowing moon. I hardly slept. When I got up at dawn, I saw my older uncle making tea in an earthen vessel. He gave me a glassful. After having it I slipped out of the house and started retracing the path that my mother and I had taken the day before. I actually managed to reach Samrala and went straight home to my grandmother.

By mid-morning, someone had arrived from my uncle's home and Dadi was told that everyone was desperately searching for me there. My mother was quite taken aback by my behaviour and thereafter she always seemed hesitant to display her love for me.

My childhood was full of dangers which I would embrace with open arms. A madman would pass our colony in Samrala and many children would run after him. I too accosted him, saying, 'I am not afraid of you.' He, in turn, told me to embrace the banyan tree. I did so and he hit me hard on my behind with his tattered shoe. Everyone started laughing. However, we continued to chase him whenever he came our way because we found his banter and manner entertaining.

I recall another danger. Some people had turned a huge shallow metal vessel into a makeshift boat as our colony was flooded during the rains. After use, it was left upside down in the shoal. We boys went there and tried to flip the vessel over to have a boat ride. I tried to lift it up from one side with my head. But it slipped and fell; I escaped death by pulling out in a fraction of a second.

One day, trying to climb a wall, I fell down on the ground and my spine hit a brick. Instead of consoling me, Dadi started to thrash me. She had a very heavy hand and her beatings hurt even more than being hit with my uncle's slipper. She then wanted to confine me in a small, dark room but her friend dissuaded her.

Dadi would often thrash my cousin in the same way. Once the boy urinated into the well and she beat him up mercilessly, shouting, 'Will you ever do this again?' When she got tired of doing so she took him to the well and, threatening to push him in, asked, 'Will you ever do this again?' The poor boy could hardly speak. So he gestured with his finger that he would never do so.

There are the injuries of the body and injuries of the mind. Yes, I remember another little pain from those impressionable days. The house across the street belonged to an army subedar. One summer the subedar came with his children to spend the vacation there. My cousin and I decided to visit them. The subedar's son's name was Amarjit and he was two years older than me. He had a big football and we asked him to let us play with it. But he broke our hearts, saying he did not wish to play with us. He was far more intelligent than us because of his army upbringing.

But the greatest sorrow of my childhood was the death of my mother's older brother. His leg got burnt and an infection set in. It spread all over his body. While he was in the hospital we would try to hold his leg down but it would quiver and shake as though it were made of rubber and had no weight at all. The day his body was brought to our home in Samrala, my younger uncle followed, weeping loudly, and I did not like the noise he was making. My older uncle had played a valuable role in nurturing a love for literature in my heart. I recall my uncle sitting on the terrace with his hookah in one hand and a book open on his lap. He would recite a kissa, or legend, from the book and then explain it to the men sitting around him. I would be playing in a corner, glad to be on vacation in my uncle's home. I did not quite know what he was saying but the magic of his voice attracted me. He had only a kissa or two in his collection and the legend of Heer–Ranjha was not one of them. Later, I found the Heer–Ranjha kissa in the cupboard of a cousin who worked as a labourer. I could not read it and my cousin told me that I would have to study some more before being able to comprehend it.

When I had first heard my uncle read from the kissa of Nar Sultan I was fascinated with the images the words created in my mind. The flower of literature had blossomed in my heart. In later years I came into contact with many poets and intellectuals who tried their best to convince me that literary values were different from the values of life. However, they were unable to do so. I still feel that life and literature are part of a harmonious whole.

Friends and Foes

When the labourer woman
roasts her heart on the griddle
the moon laughs from behind the tree,
the father amuses the younger one
making music with bowl and plate,
the older one tinkles the bells
tied to his waist and dances.
These songs do not die;
nor does the dance in the heart . . .

I had quite a few close friends—Ramdas, Malkit and Daku. One day a little girl who was gathering dung was hit by Daku's gulli (a small, flat wooden projectile used in games). Blood trickled down her forehead. The girl's uncle brought her to Daku's home to complain. His house was next to my masi's house, and I too was there that day. Daku and his family were not at home but the girl's uncle had gathered the neighbours and was pointing at her injured forehead. The girl looked at me and I looked back at her. She was beautiful—

slender, with dimpled cheeks that enhanced her rosy complexion. Her hair was parted and braided into two plaits, a few curls scattered around her forehead. I could not take my eyes off her. She became the subject of my first poem.

Daku was a very naughty boy. Of course he had not hit the girl on purpose but when he decided to be difficult even older people would tire of him. He was a little younger than me. When he tried to act naughty, I would catch hold of him but he would smile and say, 'Don't hit me, my friend.' My anger would vanish but once or twice I did hit him and I think it was because I was angry with him for wounding that beautiful girl. One day, passing the fields, I saw a strange sight. A sparrow was tied upside down to a wheat stock. When I told Daku about it, he said, 'I was the one who hung the sparrow upside down.' Sometimes he would play a prank and then jump into the pond or the stream to escape punishment. But all my friends were not like him.

Malkit studied with me from class I to class VII and then he dropped out of school. Their family was poorer than ours even though his grandfather used to mend shoes in the village and his older brother was doing some work for the landlords. We were better off than them only because my father was not a slave to any kind of addiction. Dadi would tell me that she once gave my father two annas to spend at the fair when he was a child. He went there, saw everything, but came back and put the money back in her hands. He started taking care of the cattle of a Jat Sikh family and later joined them as a labourer, getting a small share of the crop. Although the landlords were miserly, they did no injustice to my father and he was never in debt. On the other hand, Malkit's father would always get into some kind of debt because he was a spendthrift and a chain smoker. Malkit and I would often be doing sit-ups in school, as punishment. We would look at each other's muscles to see who was stronger.

Ramdas was from a family of 'mate's—a designation used colloquially for a supervisor of labourers—and although he was my uncle by relation, he was my age and so we were friends. His grandfather or great-grandfather had worked as a mate in a brick kiln and the whole family was known thus. Although Ramdas dropped out in class I, he was very good at mental maths. He was adept at playing cards and could guess what cards the opponent had. He would solve maths problems in his mind, while I found them far too tough. One day I stole a five-rupee note from home and took him along to the market to share the booty. We ate some savouries and smoked a cigarette each. Spitting paan on the way home, Ramdas said, 'You may mind, but I must tell you that it is not correct to steal money from home.' This really irked me because he had had no qualms sharing the booty but was now passing judgement.

His father smoked a hookah so Ramdas too enjoyed

sharing a cigarette with me. His nickname was Lashu. Once, when I called him by his nickname, his grandfather overheard me. Immediately, the old man pulled the hookah pipe out of his mouth and scolded me. Since then I made it a point to address him as Ramdas. He would call me Dadu and later he started calling me Lalu.

My dearest friend was Jagir, who dropped out in class III. I would rush to his house soon after school. Friends would get together in his house by the pond and play in the narrow street. The cool breeze rising from the pond and passing through the street would make us languid and sleepy. Our favourite sport was the circus game. We would go to a nearby plot with a half-built wall. Since there were no horses or monkeys at our disposal, on the very first day of the game we tied a bat on a dog's back and watched as it ran all over the town trying to shed its burden. I would take a goat from home and make her walk on the wall like the billy goat that walked on a stretched wire in the circus. We would make the goat lie down, pull her ears over her eyes and hold them in place with a shoe. The goat would lie there quietly and move only when we uncovered her eyes. Jagir had quite a temper. One day he hit his sister with a piece of lead and she started getting fits. At the slightest provocation he would roll his tongue beneath his teeth and hurl whatever he could find at his opponent. We too got into scraps a couple of times.

Were we fighting each other or was it our anger at being the children of a lesser god?

Growing up, I was constantly reminded of the vicious sting of the caste system, especially in my interactions with upper-caste folk.

My experiences with the Brahmin boys in the town, for instance, were very strange. These boys could not tolerate the lower-caste boys even looking at them when they played. One day in the playground a Brahmin boy came and hit me hard on my shin with a hockey stick carved crudely out of a tahli or hardwood branch. I had done nothing wrong; I was just standing there watching the boys play hockey. The next day, I took out my stick and blocked his path. He got scared, retraced his steps and went home another way.

One day my friend Malkit and I were running about, rolling tyres, when two boys from the goldsmith clan stopped us and challenged us to a round of wrestling. We beat them hollow. Still not satisfied, they challenged us to a fist fight. Malkit gave such a blow to one of them that he fell down. Then Malkit told me, 'Let's leave.' We beat a hasty retreat, rolling tyres all the way.

There is another incident I'd like to narrate. Often, I would get the chance to accompany cattle to remote villages on the mounds. But after some years this task came to an end. I was unhappy because I liked carrying the tall stick in my hand and playing cowherd. One day, stick in hand and looking for a cow, I reached the bazaar. There was a signboard there with a large picture of Mahatma Gandhi. Beneath it was an inscription saying that just as a pitcher of milk was ruined by a single drop of poison, a society was ruined by the malaise of untouchability. The stick in my hand was almost as tall as I was, reaching up to my ears. I held it with both hands and gave the Mahatma's picture a hard blow. Then I ran home as fast as I could. In this case, my anger can be attributed to a mistake because, as I later realized, I had misread 'untouchability' as 'untouchables'.

Once, rolling an old bicycle tyre, I crossed the bazaar street and went over to the fields where my father was working. The half-built structures there were something new to me. An Akali sitting by the structures hailed me. Giving me an eight-anna coin tied in a silk handkerchief, he asked me to fetch him a packet of Deluxe cigarettes and a matchbox. I did so and he gave me the change.

This was perhaps my first encounter with a cigarette. Earlier I used to take a drag from other people's hookahs. Later, I too started buying cigarettes to keep in my pocket, taking care to smoke them stealthily. As the addiction grew, I would smoke at night, hiding under the quilt, and would tell Dadi that the smoke was coming from the oil lamp. Since I was smoking on the sly, I tried to keep the smoke inside as long as possible and this adversely affected my health. The Lamp brand cigarette I smoked was much too strong. One day Dadi found me out. I had hidden a half-extinguished cigarette and she chanced upon it. She told me that it was a very serious matter which she would not handle herself but report to my father. She wrapped the cigarette in a rag and shoved it in the strings of her cot. I took it from there and smoked it later because she never told on me. Later she was to tell me that she had held many of my secrets close to her heart.

Some childhood memories pain me and make me repentant. Children can be very cruel and I recall how we would tease old men. One day we started hurling pebbles at an old man of the sikligar (nomadic blacksmith) clan who was sitting in his shanty. When the old man came out and started wailing, I felt very bad.

Another time, we boys troubled an old man deep in slumber in his home. We hurled pebbles at him through the window. Daku had started this nasty business. The old man came out with a spear to hit us. We hid behind the mounds. The children playing under the tahli tree got scared and started running away. Among them was my younger sister, Amro. She was running to the other side of the pond. The old man mistook her for Malkit and threatened, 'Just you wait, Malkit! I will follow you to your house and give you a sound thrashing!'

Then there was the bow-and-arrow episode that

earned me a lot of flak. The arrow in question was not the ordinary, flimsy sort which children play with during Ramlila. Instead, with a couple of coins from home, I specially got a long, sharp and strong arrow fashioned by the blacksmith. I was so fond of the arrow that I would carry it along all the time. One day I aimed it at the tahli near the pond but, afraid that it would fall into the water, I did not release it properly. So, instead of piercing the tree it pierced young Teeti's leg. I pulled it out and gave him a smaller arrow and asked him not to tell his parents what had happened. I was very fond of his family because his father and mine worked together.

But my misadventures with the arrow didn't end there. Another time, in my enthusiasm, I shot the arrow into a mud wall. The village headman was passing that way. He stopped to pull out the arrow and I went and hid myself inside the house. I could hear him talking to the neighbourhood women. Then Dadi called out, 'Why are you hiding now? Come out.' Clutching the arrow, the headman reprimanded me, 'It had dug deep into the wall. If it had hurt me, I would have been dead.' He handed me the arrow and I was happy to get it back. But he also whacked me on my ear and head. There was also an incident where the arrow pierced the upper leg of a pig and it ran away, grunting wildly. The pig sped into the lane of its master's home with the arrow still lodged in its leg. And that was the last I saw of my dear deadly weapon.

I also recall a painful prank with a peacock. After school we would sit on a tree and return to the building when all the others had left. We would roam about freely and do our homework. Often we would come early to the school and one day we found a peacock in our classroom. It was beautiful and we stood there, utterly fascinated. It was trying to get out through the ventilator. I had seen peacocks roam about on the terrace in my mother's village home and I wanted one around our home too. Daku said, 'Let's catch it.' He pounced on the peacock and called out to me to help him. The peacock struggled hard but we managed to capture it. We were carrying it home to keep it as a pet when, on the way, an older boy asked for it. Afraid that he would tell on us, we gave him the peacock. Later I learnt that peacock flesh is eaten and I felt bad about handing the bird over to him. If the older boy had asked us to set it free, I would have had no guilt on my conscience.

Running alongside these childhood memories are the imprints of other experiences. The big event of my childhood was the coming of electricity to our town. Even before electricity came, I would dance around the poles; and when it did, the lights in the bazaar left me wonderstruck. I would often roam around the bazaar just to watch the lights. I once heard the sound of a song coming from the jagirdar's home. I peeped in through the mesh window. The jagirdar's daughter was dancing in front of the radio and her anklets were jingling. But

I wasn't so fascinated by her. It was the radio that had caught my fancy, and I wanted her to move out of the way so that I could have a good look at it.

The real magic of electricity, however, was displayed before my eyes when the jagirdar's older daughter got married. It was said that a staggering sum of 1.75 lakh rupees was spent on the marriage. In those days it was a princely sum indeed. And what antics of electricity dazzled my eyes on the big wedding night! Bulbs were rotating, switching on and off and forming a myriad patterns and designs. This was something entirely new. Sadly, the marriage followed the old, beaten track. The girl was sent back to her father's house, on the third day, by her husband and his family. Her father was so shocked that he fell ill and did not come out of his house for a full month.

I was very small when the Partition riots broke out. I recall seeing two homes go up in flames but I was hardly three or four and could not understand what was happening around me. Later I heard that murder, loot and rape of the worst kind took place in and around Samrala. Wells were filled with the bodies of young girls who chose to drown themselves rather than lose their honour. The streets were strewn with corpses and it was difficult to venture outdoors. Two hoodlums who were very close to the jagirdar surrounded Muslim women. The women told them to take their valuables and spare them. The valuables were taken but the women were also raped and killed and their naked bodies were thrown in the street. Later the culprits started misbehaving with Harijan women. They kidnapped one, put her in a car and took her somewhere. There was a protest and a panchayat was called by the jagirdar. The offenders said, 'We will bring her back but give us the money to go and fetch her.' The money was given and the woman came back but the offenders were not punished in any way.

Learning a Lesson

My country has
another face
Another set
of people

The atmosphere in school was not very congenial. I was kept away from sports and cultural activities. Some teachers would treat me as an equal but, by and large, I was made to feel like an outcast. I belonged to a caste which evoked hatred in both teachers and students.

When I graduated to the higher classes, I started picking up some skills which thrilled me, like sketching. I especially liked to trace out a picture and then shade it. I traced a picture of Bhagat Ravidas which showed him standing. Below the image were a pair of shoes and some cobblers' tools. The teacher in charge of the class looked at the drawing strangely and then laughed at it with some contempt, and the students joined in. I brought the picture home.

In the junior classes, students would stage skits

in which they played the part of upper-caste Jats. I, too, longed for a chance to play those roles. Once I got a chance. I just had to be on stage as one of three policemen who drag a person from one side to the other. But the day the play was to be staged, I was thrown out of the cast. It was felt that two policemen would suffice. There was no need for a third.

I never won a prize for cleanliness, though on inspection day I would go to school after scrubbing my face hard with laundry soap and tucking my kurta neatly into my khaki shorts. Never did I, or any other boy from a lower caste, get a chance to lead the prayers at the morning assembly. We went to a school meant for all, but students from the lower castes were always made to feel inferior.

Once, a teacher was preparing three or four of us for a poetry recitation. I still remember the poem, '*Kangali deson kadhni hai / Bekari di jadh wadhni hai*' (We have to drive out poverty from our country / We have to strike at the roots of unemployment). But finally, pointing at me, the teacher said, 'Not this boy. His voice breaks.' A healthy, good-looking boy was taken in my place.

Master Harbans Lal would glare at the boys with his big, bulging eyes before thrashing them. Then he would declare, 'Do you know who I am? They call me Ravana!' He said this not just because Ravana was a Brahmin but also because he used to play Ravana every year in the local Ramlila play. He was cruel when it came to punishing his students. He would twist someone's finger or yank another's hair but he was not casteist. Once or twice we had seen him even taking dal from the homes of the Chamars. We learnt that he was very poor. It was difficult for him to send his children to school. His son had spoken to me a couple of times. For a Brahmin to be poor is not so unfortunate because people would still gladly offer them alms. But since he was associated with the much hated Ravana even the Brahmin boys felt that he was very cruel.

Master Jaidev was a short and squat man who taught me in class II. He was a strange man who resembled a round orange. He would constantly make a noise, screaming and shouting, and he wielded the stick so hard that the poor boy he was hitting would fall down. He dealt me a few blows and I got so scared that the mere thought of those thrashings made me fall ill. After I had recovered my health I refused to go to school because I hated it. There was a strange smell in the school which troubled me, and I did not want to study in the school with Master Jaidev as the tutor.

The other branch of the school was run by an old Brahmin, and I was admitted there. It was here that I started studying hard. I would learn my tables fast enough and was counted among the smart boys. The teacher had also been told not to beat me as I was of frail health. However, even this school was not without its problems. Whenever there was an inspection of the school or some function, the poor boys were treated shabbily and would be constantly reminded about their poverty. On the face of it, there was no caste prejudice but every day boys from lower-caste homes were scolded for lack of hygiene. Some boys were even beaten up because they were not well groomed. Hygiene and grooming too are a matter of affluence. Something trivial like trimming one's nails was a luxury for poor boys like us who had to labour hard at home and did not have any spare change to go to the barber. My classmate Nachattar started biting his nails in fear. Children from affluent homes would come in neat and clean clothes with their hair and nails trimmed and we would be scolded for not turning up in the same manner.

The school's other branch, where I was tormented by Master Jaidev, still haunted me. Actually, the building had been an old police interrogation centre, and who knows how many innocent people may have been tortured there in the past. That is why I always sensed this foul smell over there. The entrance had an old, black door. The rooms inside were laid out in a strange fashion and one could not find the way from one room to another easily. The ceilings and windows of the rooms were so high that we had to stand on the tables to look out of the windows. The rooms were dark even during daytime. It was as if we were sitting in a cinema hall waiting for a film to start. The whole atmosphere was eerie; this was not a place where children should learn their lessons.

The new branch of the school was in one of the more

populated colonies; even sitting in the classroom we could see people moving around outside. I learnt from the elders that this building had been specially made for a school. We played in the school and made merry. Before school hours, we would slide up and down the banister. The school had a compound and four or five teachers would be sitting there, my chacha among them. My uncle did not sit on a chair but on a cushion on the floor. I do not know why he did so—either the Brahmin teachers did not give him a chair or he chose to sit on the floor because of some ailment.

Chacha was my father's first cousin. His father had a shop in the bazaar where he sold bamboo sticks. This shop originally belonged to a Muslim before Chacha's father bought it from him. He had also got Chacha to learn weaving and tailoring from Muslim craftsmen. Later it became impossible for the Chamars to have their own shops. People would beat them up and get the shops vacated.

Chacha completed his class X and was sent far away to train as a teacher. He often told us that the people there were careful to use tongs when offering him bread because he was considered untouchable. He never discussed the many sorrows that he may have encountered because of caste prejudice. But there was one regret that sat heavily on his heart all his life. Once he had contested the local gurdwara elections. Although he had the highest number of votes he was not allowed to become the president. However, Chacha never grumbled about this grave injustice, taking it in his stride.

In my new school Chacha was very affectionate to the children; even if he had to point out a fault he would do so laughingly. I recall there was a Brahmin boy in our class whose nose was always running. He would tell him, 'Wonderful boy, your brook is always bubbling.' Then he would turn to the class and say, 'Those whose noses run have sharp minds.' Children were always flocking around him. It was because of him that I completed my class X and was encouraged to take an interest in the world around me. Long after retiring from the school, he would be seen walking around Samrala, his thick stick in hand. He said his final goodbye in 1992.

The Raasdhariyas really fascinated me. These interesting characters were itinerant folk theatre artistes; they seemed to be real sadhus, carrying their strange world with them. Their performances—brilliant feats of drama and dance—comprised a rich repertoire of plays like *Roop Basant*, *Kiranmayi*, *Puran Bhagat* and *Harishchandra*. These were familiar stories, the kind that all of us had grown up listening to; but to actually see them enacted on a stage was something different altogether.

Harishchandra was the most evocative of the lot. One day, referring to the role of Harishchandra, a boy from my mohalla mockingly said, 'You have become a Choorha, so you must resign yourself to weeping!'

This was a case of the caste hierarchy manifesting itself, because a Choorha (sweeper) is even lower than a Chamar. Truly, no other play had depicted the lives of sweepers so well. Watching it, I felt that the saga was set in the present. Harishchandra, after he donated his kingdom, was shown tending pigs, working with a basket and broom, cremating corpses for a fee and finally breaking down when his wife would not let him touch her for fear of being defiled. The play succeeded in conveying the sorrows of the lower-caste worker, wherein the character of the wife became symbolic of a culture of hatred. The play even had a love duet by a dandy sweeper couple, singing and playing hide-and-seek, basket, broom and all. These Raasdhariyas became my subject of study. I would watch them rehearsing and going about their chores all day. At night, when they put on their make-up for the performance, I would join the crowds that gathered around them.

For one whole year Ghasita Ram was the star of the stage and he would present one beautiful tableau after another. Sometimes he would show Lord Krishna among the clouds; at others we would catch a glimpse of Majnu pining for love. At times he would show a cat and its kittens nestling in a tree. The scene in which Meghnath is beheaded was shown very realistically. One day, he picked me out to play the part of Lord

Krishna but someone whispered something in his ear and he dropped me.

A month before Dussehra, the Ramlila performances would begin. I remember how Ravana would enter in the opening scene. Once Master Harbans Lal appeared on stage with such force that his sword fell from his hand and slid right down the stage. Mangal Bhagat was always picked for the role of Sita because he was fair, slim and sharp-featured. Sarup Nakka was usually depicted as an ugly woman but Mangal Bhagat was against such a representation; he said that her name actually meant a woman with very beautiful features.

The Raasdhariyas exposed me to a whole new world, one which gave me a completely different kind of education. In this way, I can say that what I was unable to learn in school I learnt outside in the school of life.

In the Crucible of College

Forlorn, I contemplate
a single thought:
that your oiled hair
would bring me salvation.

I was very keen to go to college, though everyone was against it. What use would it be to send a Chamar boy to college? The moneylender refused to give money for my admission fees. But my mother was determined. She sold her earrings, paid my fees and even bought me a bicycle. I started attending classes.

I used to be good-looking. One day, a girl in college placed her hand on her heart on seeing me and said to her friends, 'I think something's dropped out of here.' Another day, I found another girl of the BA course staring at me. She wore her hair in two plaits. In those days, girls wore their hair like that. She had a very sharp and pretty nose. I remember how, I was cycling to my friend Charan Singh's village when I saw this lovely girl cycling in the other direction. Two girls working in the fields stopped her. She got off her bicycle and the three of them started talking and laughing together. She was the daughter of the landlord of Charan's village.

Then one day I reached college to find everyone in mourning. Charan told me that that girl had died. The lovely girl with two plaits was no more. She had suffered a cerebral haemorrhage. 'She was studying when it happened, up on the terrace. She died at the hospital.'

Thereafter I started taking my writing more seriously. I wrote a rubai—a quatrain—on the uncertainty of life and read it at the weekly meeting of the college's literary club. I did not think it was much of a poem, but it became very popular and led to much jealousy.

Before that, my experience of college had been very different from that of school. I found that the professors teaching me English, Punjabi and economics treated me just as they did anyone else. They did not belittle me in any way. Our English professor used to say that even if his students did not pass the examination, they would definitely learn the English language. He used to be very particular about the pronunciation of the letter 'h'. I did well in the tests.

There was a turning point in my life when I started tutoring a young boy studying in class VIII. A cup of tea every day and a rupee every third day was my remuneration. But I was happy teaching Sitha and worked hard. In turn, he paid heed to everything I said and had a lot of regard for me.

But my classmates had not quite forgiven me that rubai, written for that lovely girl with two plaits. Annoyed by its unexpected popularity, they started excluding me from poetry meets. They could not bring her back from the dead so that she might mock me. Instead, there came another Sikh girl with two plaits. Her face was dimpled, and to me she looked just a wee bit like the girl I had fancied in college. One day, while I was teaching Sitha, she came in with her notebook and started drawing attention to herself. The power failed while she was there. It was dark, and I had a radium ring on my finger. 'What a beautiful ring,' she said, leaning over me. I could smell the pungent mustard oil in her hair. She asked me to come to her house to teach her. Since I was already a Marxist by ideology, I thought it my responsibility to teach. So I went there.

Then followed the terrible insult which was to haunt me for the rest of my life. At her home she gave me tea in a brass tumbler. But after I had finished, her mother picked it up with a pair of tongs and threw it into the stove to purify it by fire. Then she picked it up with the tongs again and dipped it into water. I felt ashamed and affronted, while the clatter of the tumbler being thrown about echoed in my ears.

About that time, I recall having lost my mental balance somewhat. I would get very agitated and I was unable to sleep at night. Staying awake, I kept smoking cigarettes and the smoke damaged my lungs. Half awake, I would feel strangely uncomfortable, as if I had bloated like a gas balloon. And there were nightmares too. A couple of times I woke up whimpering, my heart thudding wildly. On such occasions, I would wait till dawn before I could submit to sleep again. And, inevitably, I would wake up the following morning feeling heavy and fatigued, my throat parched. If I ventured out into the street, the boys would hurl unkind remarks at me and I would feel very angry. Once I even beat up the cousin of a Sikh girl and once the potter's son threw a brick at me but fortunately it missed its target. Those days I was always thinking of that girl. My ruminations were so intense that I was forever distracted. I had even left college.

Around that time, my parents found a girl from my caste for me in Bahilolpur and our engagement was fixed. A day after the engagement I ran into Sitha, who told me that the Sikh girl had asked him, 'So your master has got engaged?' This troubled me further.

To make things worse, I was sick all the time and my stomach was giving me a lot of trouble. My mother took me to Nathji, a local doctor, and he gave me a prescription for a medicine which the wayside peddler sold from his wares spread out under an open umbrella. I felt much better after taking it and started meeting some poet friends. But at times I was consumed by fits of anger and my family started thinking that I would have to be kept in chains. However, I was not a mental patient. There was some illness in my body which was taking its toll on my mind. I would try to write poetry during this period but was too confused to do so. One side was pulling me towards love and romance for the opposite sex while the other was tugging me towards Marxism and revolution.

It was Chacha who convinced the others in my family not to keep me in chains because, as he pointed out, it would only cause my condition to deteriorate further. Instead, I was taken some thirty kilometres away to a mental hospital. The hospital building was in a large enclosure and I saw mentally disturbed girls running around in the compound, holding their cots above their heads. Someone was standing close to the doctor, saying, 'This poor man is also ravaged by alcohol.'

The doctor received me very warmly and asked, 'Why are you wearing this kara?'

I shot back, 'I also smoke.'

The doctor then questioned me, 'Why are you wearing this blue turban?'

I retorted, 'My hair is cut short.'

Perhaps I was trying to establish my secular identity. The doctor learnt that I was a poet and started calling me 'Kavishar'. He gave me a paper and pencil and asked me to write a poem. I scribbled a few lines. The doctor then wanted to know something about the Punjabi Suba agitation which was in full swing in Amritsar at that time. Finally the doctor told Chacha that I would be cured easily with medicine.

The treatment worked. It helped me, and my physical and mental state started improving. I realized I was happy that I was engaged to be married. Life, which had been spiralling out of control, now seemed to be falling back into place again.

On the Wings of Poetry

The evening wears its familiar colours
the footpaths are walking to the basti
the lake is returning from the office
after being shunted out of work
the lake is quenching its thirst for water
the city is walking towards the villages

After I had recovered from my wretched mental and physical state, I started looking out for writers and for literary groups. This brought me close to Sukhdev Madhopuri. He used to organize the annual poetry symposium. He would collect funds and, in the process, make quite a packet for himself; but he organized the function rather well. The sad thing about this symposium was that he would make the local poets sit in the front row without allowing them to recite their poems. I had thought that this would not be my lot but the same treatment was meted out to me a couple of times. Finally, the local poets decided that Madhopuri should be replaced as the coordinator of the writers' group. I was made the secretary and functioned from the Indo-Russian Friendship Association office at Ludhiana, although this only lasted for three months. Things went wrong when a couple of writers came to spend a night in the office. One of them was accompanied by a woman whom he introduced as his sister-in-law. I was unaware that rules did not permit any man to stay with a woman. I allowed them to stay the night, and only later did I realize my folly.

I found that some writers were jealous of me. They always talked ill of me behind my back or put words in my mouth which had never been uttered. *Preetlarhi* had just published a poem of mine, and the poets were mocking me. This was a time when I was back to writing poetry and my poems were appreciated at various symposia. Assorted magazines were publishing my poems and I was steadily carving a distinctive niche for myself, although my literary peers weren't always encouraging.

Once, Kanwal, a celebrated leftist novelist, was invited for a literary gathering. We had all sat down for a meal. I was reaching out for a jug of water when Kanwal pulled the jug away as though only he had the right to drink that water. Or did our famous Marxist writer have a caste prejudice? I can't say. But I do recall Kanwal staring at me rather strangely. Perhaps his attitude reflected that . . .

Harjit Singh Mangat belonged to a landed family that had migrated from Pakistan, where, he used to say, they went to the fields in their own buggy. His grandfather was a subedar in the British Indian Army who had been given land in recognition of his brave service. But Partition changed everything for Mangat's family. I was saddened to hear that his father often hit his mother with a leather whip. At the time of Partition, when they had to run away at a moment's notice, he had screamed at his wife, 'Stop washing these clothes or you will be washed away!' She was Mangat's father's second wife; the first one had died. Mangat used to call her daughter Baljit Bhainji. Mangat's grandparents lived separately. Baljit Bhainji was a very kind girl, always taking care of Mangat and his friends and serving them lassi.

Mangat had a love–hate relationship with me. At times, he would say, 'We have tried hard to cure Lal Singh Dil of his illusions.' He was always worried that I would once again fall into the trap of my imagined romances: the Sikh girl in the college, the daughter of the landlord, the Samrala Jat girl. He would try to free my mind of these tangles.

Then something happened that ruined my peace of mind. My engagement with the girl from Bahilolpur was called off.* The very mention of Bahilolpur would

* The engagement was called off because news had somehow reached the girl's family that Dil was not keeping sound health. This rejection would haunt him for the rest of his life.

remind me of my broken engagement, and I would feel distraught. Nevertheless, Mangat advised me to take admission in Bahilolpur where the Teachers' Training Centre had just started. He even gave me thirty rupees for my expenses. I was grateful for his help. And fortunately, I got admission there.

I had joined the course fully aware that I would have to face many problems. Surprisingly, the first year passed so smoothly that I didn't even know when the time flew by. But the second year was quite another story. So many problems arose that I could not complete the course.

The primary reason for this setback was that I was unable to form any sort of friendship with any girl. In fact, the girls there mocked me and reminded me of my lower-caste status. I became extremely troubled since my mind would obsessively cling to these insults. Such thoughts unwittingly took me back to the humiliation I had suffered in the name of love and romance. All this fuelled my general awkwardness about interacting with girls. Take this, for instance. We had gone to play a football match. After an evening of revelry, we learnt the next morning that we would be playing against the team that had been winning for several years. I did what I could in the match and really ran about; but when I slowed down I heard a call, 'What's the matter?' Noticing that the rival team was being cheered by girls, I said without thinking, 'If we had girls for cheerleaders even we would have scored a dozen goals.' But later,

I felt so embarrassed by this remark that I did not go to collect the certificate even though we had won by a single goal.

Other incidents further compounded the situation. Once the headmaster's daughter and a boy from my caste were cycling when they collided head-on with each other. It happened outside the shops and was unintentional. However, the headmaster beat up the boy mercilessly with a stick. This was enough to kill my joy.

Another day, a local landlord beat up a low-caste boy. The women of the boy's family were weeping. I took the boy on my bicycle to the hospital nearby. I think this turned many people against me.

Then occurred another incident which proved to be too much for me. I had a friend named Surinder who, like me, enjoyed reading and writing poetry. He belonged to Bahilolpur. One day he asked me to write a letter which he wanted to give to a girl. After two days, there was a furore because the girl had reported the matter and there was to be an urgent meeting. This was worrisome because all the teachers were unionists too. After that I strongly suspected that a man with a stick was shadowing me, waiting to beat me up as I passed by on my cycle. Another time, a tractor passed by me, dangerously close. The third time, in the fading light of the evening, I saw someone pulling out a knife to attack me but I quickly rode away.

To tell the truth, I could not quite adjust in

Bahilolpur and probably the root cause was my earlier broken engagement.

———❦———

In Bahilolpur, I read a lot of irrelevant Russian literature. Thousands of pages on Leninist thought as well as the four thick volumes of *And Quiet Flows the Don*. It was literary, but I couldn't quite comprehend the writer's philosophy. I read many such books. The Russians had found a fine way of selling their waste paper to Indian buyers.

But I kept writing poetry and became active at literary meetings. At a function in the Bahilolpur school, I read my poem written on Vietnam. It was called 'Murdey' (Corpses).

Those who walk to Vietnam
Turn into walking, living corpses;
They are no longer
Brother, father, son or lover.

The girls were sitting in the back row and the headmaster's daughter was among them. A remark from them travelled to my ears even on the stage: 'Those who are corpses will be corpses!'

Perhaps the poem's title had indicated to the girls that I would be speaking of some unhappy leftist philosophy. But the purpose behind my writing this poem was something else. Earlier, in class one day, Master Pandit Bihari Lal had heard my poem 'Radium da Geet' (Song of Radium) and had launched on some unnecessary thematic criticism of the poem. He was a romanticist who used to close his eyes in ecstasy and sing a sentimental song by Shiv Kumar. My poem 'Murdey' was a direct attack on such uncalled-for sentimentality in the name of poetry. I had satirized poets who put together a rhyme or two and suffixed their names with those of Bulle Shah or Farid. Farid had once said, *'Birha, tu Sultan'*—longing, you reign supreme. But he had never wailed or wept in his verses.

I am criticizing poets of this kind on ideological grounds. I feel duty-bound to do so because many old manuscripts had been changed for the worse. Those days Loona, the famous heroine of the popular legend of Puran Bhagat, was addressed as Chamaran and a new dimension was given to her character in a long poem by Batalvi. However, I made an intervention of sorts in this regard. Since she was from the town of Chamba, I renamed her Chambaran.

Although there was no overt discrimination against me on the basis of caste in the college, Brahminism still made its oppressive presence felt and it became hard for me to live in the town. Then, just before the final examination, I dropped out of the Basic Training Course because I was ill-prepared for the examination.

I had been to Delhi once and planned to go there a second time. My friend Iqbal Kang had lived in Delhi and was now a truck driver. He would often tell me stories about Delhi and make it a point to condemn our Punjabi poet Amrita Pritam on one pretext or another. He said that she was a woman of capitalist ideology and would have no time for my poetry.

When I went to Delhi, poets met me very warmly. This was because they had read my poem in *Preetlarhi*. I did not meet Amrita Pritam; but, when I returned, I came to know that she had published my poem on the title page of her *Naagmani* magazine. The poem was 'Eh Vesvavan Trimatan' (These Fallen Women).

Even the prominent poets of Delhi were happy to see me and Tara Singh was one of them. I had the opportunity of sitting with him in the famous coffee house in Connaught Place and discussing literature. One evening he asked me whether I would like to visit Amrita Pritam's home but, under the negative influence of my friend Kang, I declined the invitation.

Iqbal even went to the extent of cautioning my hosts in Delhi that my stay there could lead to a police inquiry or harassment. So I had to cut short my visit and return to Samrala. During my earlier trip to Delhi, I had been introduced to Bishan Singh Upasak at a literary gathering. Upasak had looked at me and said, 'Who is this rabbit?' I was quick to reply, 'And who is this leopard?' Upasak quickly embraced me and said, 'I never say anything to rabbits.' At one poetry reading, we were all given thirty rupees each. Upasak gathered all this money and bought liquor and we had a merry time drinking and dancing on the footpaths of Delhi. He would raise the glass to me, recite a couplet and gulp the drink down. Upasak looked like a handsome actor or a well-groomed worker of the Congress party.

Kang had also introduced me to Sansar Singh Gharib and Kulwant Singh Virk. Virk was quite a character. Once he bought a packet of jalebis and we walked a long distance eating the sweets. Suddenly, he pulled me to the pavement saying I should not be run over by a car because I still had to eat more jalebis.

There were also some awkward moments in the company of my dear friends. Once, for instance, when I had gone to Ludhiana, my friend Hardeep let loose some lumpens on me in a cinema hall. One of them was called Jeet, and the name immediately reminded me of the Sikh girl from college. The memory still pained me.

Another time, the teachers in Samrala sent me with a girl called Lalita to an office to submit some papers. Kang was also accompanying us. We stopped at a shop to have tea and Kang slipped away before paying the bill. The shopkeeper threatened me, saying that I would have to take off my pyjama if I did not pay up. I was upset by Kang's behaviour and went to another friend, Dharma, to get some money. Dharma too felt that Kang had not done the right thing.

In Samrala, I recall the whole mohalla talking about Nehru. Chacha went to the extent of calling him 'Panditji'. He would say, 'And then Panditji wore his black coat.' He wanted to convey that in spite of not being a practising lawyer Nehru felt compelled to take up some special case.

There was a big poster of Nehru hanging on the wall of Chacha's living room. This may have been so because he needed to cover the mud walls of his room with paper, but he was also a supporter of the Congress. Early one morning, I read something on this poster and asked Chacha to explain it to me. But Chacha said that he would not like to see Nehru's face in the morning. 'Why?' I asked. 'A Brahmin had betrayed Guru Gobind Singh and the Shahibzadas were captured by the Sirhind Nawab.'

Now, the Chamars had been given a new status with the name of Harijan and that is why they considered themselves close to the Congress. But the situation in the temple was the way it had always been. The priest would caution the Chamars and the Balmikis by saying, 'Do not come in front, do not make any offering. It is the day of the Goddess. She will get angry!'

⟨———⟩

I had to go through more agony and it was certainly due to some spell cast by Brahminism. It was like standing on the edge of a cliff and suddenly being pushed over the brink.

In such a condition, I would see a girl pass me by, acknowledging my misery but not stopping to help me overcome it. She was a schoolteacher in a nearby village. I became obsessed. She started haunting me all the time, so much so that I was unable to do any work. If I tried to type, my fingers would just type out her name again and again. Sometime ago, a teacher met me at a poetry symposium and he would often talk about her. He told me that she always greeted his wife with an embrace. When he told me this I felt that a message was being conveyed to me. Inspired, I wrote:

You embrace someone else and show it to someone else
It is like sending a message from one to the other.

I wrote long letters to my writer friend Prem Prakash, expressing my agony over this woman. He told me to somehow pull myself together. Against all odds, I was able to do so. This was an achievement because, in the past, I had never been able to get out of such a situation.

But whenever I saw her, my mind would start playing games once again. Recently I saw her walking with a man. I thought he was her husband because he was striding ahead and she was having trouble keeping pace with him. As she passed me she said, 'He is such a bastard . . .' She repeated this line three times. If I had remained silent, I would have fallen sick once more. So I too said three times, 'What do you want?' I felt light, as though I had rid myself of a ghost for all time.

───❖───

I had written a poem called 'Des' which strongly criticized war and the notion of borders. It was generally appreciated. But when I sent it to several magazines, none published it. It was finally published much later in my anthology and in *Lakeer*. But sadly, it was not published when I first wanted it to be.

A new magazine asked for a poem but, to my misfortune, the editor misplaced it. Prof. Sahni, who had taught me in college, was teaching Punjabi in the new college that opened in Samrala. He was invited to become a member of our literary group and I read out this poem there. Prof. Sahni said, 'The poem is beautiful.' But soon after, he slipped a currency note out of his pocket and gave it to the president of our group, saying that he would keep sending the membership fee but would not attend the meetings. After this he left, smiling.

I later read the same poem at a function in Samrala and felt very happy.

───❖───

I had not been able to understand the country's politics from 1962 to 1965, but after reading some literature and talking to people I could somewhat comprehend it. I also read some Chinese literature in English. But it had so many dates and references that I could not make much of it. I also tried, without success, to lay my hands on *The Untold Story,* where the controversial Gen. Brij Mohan Kaul, a distant kinsman of Pandit Nehru who resigned after the debacle of 1962, told his version of the events in the Sino-Indian conflict.

So one day I asked a senior member of the Communist Party to explain to me the politics of the time. He shrugged his shoulders and said, 'I feel that all the dictators of the world are getting together.' I then got a chance to talk to a member of the Communist Party (Marxist) and the smart fellow said in a questioning tone, 'When China attacked India, who sent them back?'

I had still not found the right answer to my question. It was while chatting with Kulwant Neelon, a fellow writer, that I first learnt about the meeting between Nehru and Mao. Kulwant never needed to be prodded for information since he was in the habit of waxing eloquent on his own.

This bit of news was a serious matter, and a debate was raging on the issue. Fundamentalist Hindu Congressmen would constantly harp on this topic and then accuse others in the party of toeing Mao's line. Many people saw this as an opportunity to end Marxism once and for all. On the other hand, the Russians too had vested interests in the matter. No one was making an effort to bring peace between the two neighbouring countries at war. Everyone clearly had their own agenda in such a serious political development.

Even before our literary group came under the influence of the Cultural Revolution, I had read a book which had thrown open the doors and windows of my mind. This book was essentially a dialogue between Chinese and Russian political cadres, exchanged by way of letters. Reading it, I became convinced that the Russians were trying to oppress the others just as the landlords had oppressed us.

One influential member of our literary group, Pandit Om Prakash, had wanted us to frame a resolution against China for desecrating temples and other religious buildings. I said, 'So what?' The meeting was never called and we passed no such resolution.

During that time I wrote a poem called 'Nadeen' (Weeds) which was an ode to Chairman Mao. This poem was published by *Lakeer* and I forgot all my grudges against the magazine.* At the time, Mao was a favourite topic of discussion on the college campus where I was studying. One girl would say that Mao had replaced his own eyes with the eyes of some girl. Another would chip in, 'So what? I would not

---

* It is possible that some of the poems that Dil had previously sent to this magazine had been turned down. That would explain the grudge he mentions here.

mind giving my eyes to someone.' The argument heated up and one boy picked up a weight from the college canteen and, asking everyone to imagine that it represented Mao, said, 'Now just try and touch it.'

I also got an invitation to read my poem at Gurusar Sudhar College during a function organized by a writer named Sukhminder Rampuri. The college was a hotbed of political activity. As my name was announced, I got up to recite my poem 'Athan' (Evening Tide) when the students started laughing. This was done in good humour, and they were not trying to heckle or belittle me in any way. So I smiled and responded that the evening poem could well be heard in the afternoon too. The principal got up and gave a little speech on the art of listening to poetry.

At that time if someone had asked me what exactly the Cultural Revolution was all about, I would have found it difficult to give an adequate answer. But the real question was whether a political revolution would come first or would another sort of churning, like the Cultural Revolution in China, show the way instead.

Naxalbari, Here I Come

Remember that day
when your waters caressed
my shoulders,
and
I felt a gun had been placed there

The news of Naxalbari spread like wildfire. Those days I was working as a labourer on daily wages. I carried heavy loads up and down a ladder, and all this activity gave me a strange energy. I felt I would now be able to accomplish what I could have achieved had I been present during the upsurge in Vietnam. I felt I was on the threshold of realizing the imminent Revolution.

One of those days I was standing outside a liquor shop when Harbans Lal arrived. He was from a landowning family and was always arguing with me that I should accept him as a comrade. I was not the office-bearer of any group so I do not know why Harbans wanted me to acknowledge his status as a comrade. He used to work in an electrical repair shop and managed to get some money from there. He called out to me, 'Come, Comrade. Let us drink our fill.' There were two or three men with him. As we were drinking he began talking about Naxalbari—a topic I was passionate about. Consequently, I started speaking loudly. Finally I got tired and said I wanted to go home, and he specially ordered half a bottle for me, saying I could drink it at home since I was leaving early. I was already quite high and I drank the half-bottle neat in one go. All I can remember after that is when I tried to get up holding on to the table, I fell down. The next day I found myself bruised all over, and my clothes were blood-stained.

I later learnt that Harbans and his friends had put me in a rickshaw and sent me home. However, the rickshaw-wallah dropped me midway and a few boys who were standing there took me to the landlord's house. I entered the big house raising slogans about Naxalbari and was beaten up near the big drain and thrown there. My cousin found me there the next morning. My mother went to the landlord's home and asked them apologetically if I had teased his daughters. This question could have started another row but fortunately the girls said that nothing of the kind had happened. This was the same house where I used to watch the little girl dancing to the music of the radio in my boyhood.

Sometime later, when I had been laid off from work, I took up a job in the patwari's shop where I met a full-time worker of the Communist Party (Marxist). It was here that I also came across the tall and impressive Babu Ram Vairagi.

Thereafter, I was engaged in the work of pasting posters on the Naxalbari movement all over the town. Babu Ram Vairagi was collecting a list of names of people in favour of the movement. He made the mistake of printing these posters from the Khooni Inquilab Press and got Mangal Singh, a tailor, and another innocent person to sign them. The police seized the posters from the press and took Mangal Singh and the other man to the police station. There they were hung upside down. The two fellows had no choice but to apologize and return home. Thus, we lost two sympathizers to the cause.

At the time, Comrade Mal Rampuri and I prepared the manifesto for the Inquilabi Likhari Sabha. We took this manifesto to many writers, especially the younger ones. We even went looking for you, Amarjit Chandan, but you were not there. We went to Talban to meet Ravinder and one other writer but they were also not there. However, the people we met promised us full support. Rampuri and I were trying to organize writers to be part of a common revolutionary forum by way of a magazine, the manifesto of which stated that we would establish contact with writers of other languages too. We sent out this manifesto to the newspapers and Rampuri and I were its temporary office-bearers. China had not recognized any Indian revolutionary or writer but the news of this revolutionary writers' front was announced on Radio Beijing.

———

As part of my work for the Naxalbari movement, I spent two months in Mandi Ahmadgarh with Comrade Des Raj. Although he was a trader he had a carefree nature like Chacha's. The difference between the two was that Des Raj was always laughing while Chacha rarely did so. Des Raj used to wear a long kurta and loose-fitting pyjamas. He was tall and broad and had the look of a wrestler. Once, when he casually asked a passerby if all was well, the man replied, 'It is good when the days pass peacefully.' To this Des Raj laughed and said, 'What about the days that don't pass so?'

It was a wonder how Des Raj remained cheerful despite the ordeals he'd suffered. His right hand had been amputated because it had been burnt badly. There was a story behind this. One day some dacoits entered his house and demanded the keys of the lockers. Des Raj refused to comply, so they lit a fire and put his hand in it. Frightened, his mother immediately handed over the keys to them.

Des Raj enjoyed sharing his lunch with me in the same bowl. He would pour dal and curd into one bowl, and we would dip pieces of roti into that mix and happily eat together. This simple ritual made me feel that the two of us shared a close bond. This was the time when we printed and pasted more posters.

A peculiar incident comes to mind of the time I stayed in Mandi Ahmadgarh. While living there, I would sometimes visit Vairagi's village. Once, when I boarded the train to go there, I found that it was really crowded. There was a young girl standing next to me, holding her books to her breast. Due to the crush of people, I was almost pressed against her. I got off at the next station. While crossing the station to go to the other side, I noticed that the girl briefly raised her lowered eyes and looked at me. Then she was gone.

After Mandi Ahmadgarh, my next destination was Comrade Chetan's farm. Vairagi took me there. Chetan put me to work in the fields. His son also worked with me. This field was near the Satluj River. Father and son would argue with each other as they worked. They also distilled a raw country spirit which we would drink in the fields as we discussed what the role of the comrades should be. Here I came across Comrade Mal who had seven sons and five daughters. Comrade Mal was an old man and none of his dozen children was married. His oldest daughter was greying and bent. Comrade Vairagi often came there and he would have heated arguments with Comrade Mal. And Comrade Harnek Singh Vaid, who had a shop in Mullanpur, would also come there and engage in long conversations with Chetan and his wife.

Comrade Chetan was full of praise for his eldest

daughter and would narrate many stories about her. One day, I recited my new poem to her. The poem was called 'Lal Purav' (Red East). I was planting corn another day, a task I had never done before. She came there and said, 'If you did not know how to do it, you should have called me.' Together we completed the task.

As far as love goes, I feel it is a meeting of souls. Nothing came out of this association because the girl had probably learnt about my past and my caste from some of my relatives when she accompanied us to Samrala looking for a job. But her kindness travelled a long way with me and came to my aid when I was alone or in danger.

And danger often had a way of finding me. I was once carrying a message of the comrades from one village to another when I saw a few policemen looking my way suspiciously. It was a moonlit night, and I went and stood in the shade of a tree. The policemen were probably looking for liquor and did not bother to follow me. Another night I was asked to deliver food in the fields. When I retraced my footsteps the following day, I saw that I could easily have fallen into a well on the way.

On yet another night I was passing through a dark street in the village when a pack of dogs surrounded me. Sensing danger, my hands reached for the pistol I was carrying in my pocket but the dogs suddenly ran away without even barking. That night I attended a meeting of a hundred comrades along with Comrade Chetan and Comrade Vairagi. The senior comrade from Mahal Kalan was also there. He had earlier asked for one of my poems to have it published in a magazine. A few days ago, I had written a poem, 'Kangla Teli', and had recited it several times. I had also sent it to some magazines for publication. I recited some verses from this poem to Santokh Singh Dhir, who twisted his mouth in irritation and said, 'What is this? I cannot understand anything.' Instead of asking me to recite it, Vairagi seized the notebook from me and read it himself.

Those days a strike was on at the Birla Seed Farm in Ropar. The thanedar (sub-inspector) of the Chamkaur Sahib police station had built a false case of theft against Comrade Hardev Singh, and he had been mercilessly beaten up in custody. We learnt many stories of the thanedar's cruelty. Comrade Hardev Singh was in hospital and his arm was badly fractured. A meeting was held to plan a revenge against this thanedar. The names of thirteen volunteers were listed and I was to be one of them. We were to carry arms and ammunition hidden in rolls of bedding—at that time I used to sleep in the woods near the Satluj. And so we all gathered in an orchard near the Chamkaur Sahib police station before assembling in a room near the tube well.

It then struck me that in everyone's life there comes a moment of choice. At that time Comrade Gurmukh Singh Lalton of the Desh Bhagat Yadgar Hall fame had sent a message saying I should start working for him. He even offered to provide me a bicycle. But I came here instead.

The next evening the son of a Border Security Force (BSF) officer and I were to find out whether the thanedar was in his quarters or in the police station. We roamed about for an hour to fulfil this task. I was carrying a pistol but my companion was not carrying any weapon. We learnt that the thanedar was in the police station. We reported this to the other prominent comrades and then the plan for the attack was made. This was our strategy: two of us were to go inside to lodge a report and the rest would follow. One person would have been enough to tackle the thanedar but they wanted us to carry away all the arms and ammunition available in the police station.

There was one problem, however: we had only twelve weapons. So it was decided that the thirteenth weapon would be seized from a policeman on duty. Unfortunately the guard on duty was not carrying a gun. So it turned out that I was the only one who was going in without a weapon.

At least four people in our group were agents who acted as informers; the others had not been allowed to meet one another. Two volunteers, a young army man called Lakhwinder and the second a son of a police official, entered the police station. Eleven of us were waiting outside. As soon as we heard a shot fired, we quickly assembled in the compound of the police station. The path to the building as well as the compound were covered with wild akk growth. Babu Ram Vairagi had been the first one to enter the station. The revolutionaries kept firing from outside. After some time Vairagi and the police official's son returned. The latter told us that while Lakhwinder was dictating his report, a constable hit him hard on the head with a stick and he fell down. He did not tell us what else had happened inside. Later, we learnt from the police that the chowkidar had been beaten up.

While the others who had entered the station now rushed out, I thought I heard a shot being fired from inside the building. Immediately, I retreated a little towards the akk plants. Vairagi ordered a roll call and realized that there were only twelve of us as Lakhwinder was still inside.

Amar Acharwal asked, 'What should we do now?'

Vairagi said, 'We have to take a decision whether we should re-enter the police station or not.'

From what we had been told it seemed that Lakhwinder had dropped dead. I wondered if there was any point in carrying a dead body while we were running to save our lives. I realized that our leadership was now in panic and I was carrying no weapon. Earlier, I had been abusing the policemen but was now silent like the others.

Irritated, I said, 'Let us enter the building at once or we should move away.'

Acharwal said, 'It is best to move away.'

However, we did not run away like cowards. In fact, I took Baldev's Sten gun to make up for not having had the fortune of getting the guard's rifle. I loaded two rounds of bullets. Tara Singh Chalaki and Ujagar Singh Lalton were also in our group. We all gathered in a mango orchard and, inevitably, began to discuss the events that had taken place in the police station. It was then that we were able to piece together what had actually transpired.

When the first two comrades entered the station to lodge a complaint stating that their bicycle had been stolen, the guard on duty had asked a constable to write down the report. But, when Vairagi entered the police station the policemen got suspicious. Bhinder fired three rounds and the thanedar screamed and fell down. The guard who was standing behind the thanedar received some bullet injuries in his shoulder.

But the gravity of the situation was not lost on any of us. That night, it was decided that we would all depart in separate directions so that no one would know where the other had gone.

Two of us took a train to Khanna. By the following morning, everyone was talking about the attack on the Chamkaur Sahib police station. We heard people discussing the incident at a tea shop. One man said that they must have gone there to get rifles and another retorted, 'What else would they get there? A bag of sugar?'

My companion and I parted ways there. I roamed

around and, one day, visited Baldev's home only to learn that the police had raided it. His mother and sister, standing behind a curtain, looked very unhappy. I then boarded a bus going to Kharar. On the way it stopped at a railway crossing and I saw some people getting off. But they soon returned with a couple of policemen, so I quickly jumped off the bus and disappeared into the fields by the road. I walked some two miles through the fields before gathering courage to cross the road. I had to stop myself again because I noticed a police tent close by, but somehow I managed to slink away.

My relatives had got to know that I was wanted by the police. The police had raided our Samrala home. I reached my dadi's village, Manaki, and found a lot of people gathered there. Dadi's older nephew asked me to leave quickly because the police could come any time. This was because Gurdev, Dadi's younger nephew, had killed his wife. They had been quarrelling ever since Gurdev had returned from his job in the army.

So again I took to the road. On the way back to Ludhiana, a motorcyclist gave me a lift for a substantial part of the journey. I spent the night in his village, Ramgarh. I then visited another comrade, Ranjit, and together we went to Acharwal's village. At that time, we were also a part of another operation. We were to capture the land of an army captain. But when we reached there, we found that all the labourers were out of their shanties and the land was being ploughed.

Acharwal ordered, 'Start firing.' I disagreed because I felt we would not achieve anything by opening fire.

I went up to the workers and said, 'Listen, friends, this land was to be captured today but very cleverly the landlord has sent you to plough it so that we should get into an altercation with you and he save his land. I promise you that when the land is divided, half of it will be given to you and half of it will be given to the villagers.'

The old man did not say anything but he gestured to the others to move the oxen-pulled plough out of the field. I started raising slogans: 'Long live the revolutionary tillers of the soil!' They must have heard these slogans as they retreated to the village. Someone was operating a tractor on the southern side, and he remained oblivious until we all walked up to him. I said, 'Fire bullets into the tyres of his tractor.' At this, he quickly drove the tractor away.

A dust storm soon started. The sky was red with dust and the comrades rushed to take shelter. I was left in the fields with just one boy called Lal Sekhon who had had his hair shorn a few days earlier. We did not even have a bicycle. We thought that we would be captured by the police because a police jeep had been doing the rounds of that area.

We could hear songs blaring from a loudspeaker in the village. The loudspeaker was hung on a neem tree. So we decided to go there and join the crowd that had gathered there for what seemed to be a wedding. We told the head of the family the truth. The old man said, 'Never mind, come and join us. Our son too had gone to the meeting of you comrades today.'

It turned out that the function was actually an engagement party. We were taken up to the terrace and seated with the guests. We were served food and the person who had brought our thalis wanted to know if we would like to drink some liquor. I was quick to reply that we were comrades and did not drink liquor. There is great pride in professing one's comrade identity and I am experiencing this again as I put these words on paper.

Early in the morning, we had a cup of tea and moved on to hear some sad tidings. Bujha Singh, Daya Singh and Hari Singh Mirdangpuri had been killed by the police.

I recall the first time I met Comrade Bujha Singh. Dressed in khadi, with a sweater that had holes in it, he was always seen carrying a book of Lenin's writings with him. He had a carefree nature and he inspired all of us with his anecdotes.

In Custody

Someone's eyes must be
reaching out to the evening
Eyes lit with hope must be
glued to the river bank
O, Autumn Wind!
Take my greetings and say:
'One should never lose heart
thus for anyone's sake'

Those were tough times indeed. Every day, we would hear of one encounter or another. I started feeling that I would be killed in one such fake encounter. Comrade Chetan was arrested by the police. His son probably heaved a sigh of relief.

I was sitting with a companion in a lane a little away from the bazaar. The lane was deserted and no children were out playing. Just then a police jeep entered the lane; some policemen got down and came towards me. I promptly started raising slogans: 'Naxalbari Zindabad, Inquilab Zindabad!' I did so with a view to attract a crowd so that we would not be killed or taken away stealthily. The policemen raised their guns and one of them caught hold of my arm and dug a pistol into my spine.

'What is the matter?' I said. 'Why don't you fire at me? There is no need to poke me with the pistol.'

'We will fire when the time comes,' said one of them in response.

Already well acquainted with the ways of the police, I told them, 'Do not malign me by slapping a false case of opium or cocaine on me.'

'Do not worry,' he retorted. 'We will charge you with the possession of an unlicensed pistol.'

I was taken to the local police station and locked up alone in a cell. I had not yet reached the point of completely hating the police. In fact, on account of many personal experiences, I still thought they were better than many comrades.

I paced up and down the lock-up like a wounded tiger. The men in the lock-up opposite mine stared at me rather strangely. After a while, I calmed down and tried to accept the fact that I had been arrested. I felt better.

One constable passing by asked me, 'Do you want some tea?'

I said, 'So, you can speak! I thought your mouth is sealed by your beard.'

Just then another policeman came with handcuffs. I put my hands outside the bars and asked him to handcuff me. He opened the lock-up and did so. I was put in a jeep and taken to the quarters behind the army tents. These were similar to the government official's quarters; I had once spent a night with a friend in such a place. But instead of furniture, children's books or kitchen utensils, this quarter had police uniforms and belts hanging all over the place. It must have been five in the evening and there were a large number of policemen inside. A while ago the Punjab police had created a special squad to deal with the Naxalbari revolutionaries and Deputy Superintendent of Police Pannu was heading this special squad. This squad had policemen predominantly from the upper castes— Brahmins and Jats.

Still handcuffed, I was tied to a cot. One police officer started interrogating me: 'What is your name?'

'Lal Singh.'

'Father's name?'

'Raunki.'

'Village?'

'Don't assume I will answer everything you ask.'

A policeman went into the courtyard and brought in Comrade Vaid Mullapur, who had been captured along with me. This comrade would often come to visit Comrade Chetan and sit there, talking for hours. He was so fond of talking that he would cycle long distances to meet the Naxalbari revolutionaries simply to engage in passionate conversation. Sometimes he would get so excited in the course of the discussion that he would start tapping his feet as though he were dancing. The comrades too would visit him at Mullapur. But now he was sitting across me, silent, his face inscrutable like a riddle.

DSP Pannu made his way menacingly towards me. 'So how are you?' he quipped. 'I am very fine,' I replied.

Grabbing hold of my head, his hands covering my ears, he hurled me on to the cot. Then he started lashing me mercilessly with a leather strap that was used on animals. I tried to get up, but his whip came down heavily on me repeatedly. I shouted at the policemen, the words tumbling out of my mouth, but Comrade Vaid raised his finger and motioned me to remain quiet. At one point I stood up but was immediately lashed across my shoulder and the left side of my skull. I felt I was a water balloon and someone was repeatedly hitting that balloon. I was covered in blood. Barely conscious, I saw Pannu ask for a glass of water to wash the blood that had spattered on to his hands. After that I had no choice but to throw myself on the floor as the world began to spin round and round before my eyes.

'He won't tell the name of his village, this bloody Chamar!' Pannu mumbled.

Finding my voice, I said, 'I challenge you to get me to reveal the name of my village.'

I was taken to a corner of the high-walled courtyard where a table and some chairs were laid out. They pushed me on to a stool in front of the DSP. After some time a glass of tea and a bowl of sugar were placed on the table before me. The DSP said, 'Drink this tea.'

I said I never drank tea alone.

He replied, 'Have it; it has been bought with your money.' I then recalled that my pockets had been searched in the lock-up and they had found some three and a half rupees.

I told him that it did not matter whether the tea was bought with my money or not; I never drank tea alone.

Hearing this, he poured half the tea into a cup and pushed the glass towards me. I did not feel like having the tea but from the way he was drinking it I could make out that it was not too hot. I started sipping the tea. I was trying to decide what to do next but I couldn't focus. My thoughts seemed to be flying far away in different directions, and a deep sadness was descending on me. I noticed that the DSP had a pencil in his hand and some white papers were lying before him. He may have been holding a pen instead. I'm not sure because, at that time, my eyes were glued to the paper while my mind worked furiously, trying to figure out what was going on. I was very afraid of telling lies so I wanted to say nothing at all. Secondly, I wanted to break his ego.

He said, 'Tell me your name.'

I said, 'Lal Singh.'

'Father's name?'

'Raunki.'

'Village?'

'I have already endured a thrashing for this,' I answered.

He said, 'Why so? We know the name.'

I said, 'I will acknowledge you as the person in charge of the special squad if you will get me to utter the name of my village.'

He looked at the police officers standing around us and they took me inside the room. I was given one slap after another. Then they roared, 'Will you utter its name?'

I said, 'Never!'

They placed me on the cot, making me lie down on my stomach. One constable had pulled the handcuff forward and another was holding on to the hair on my head. A weight was placed on my ankles and my legs were doubled up. It was dizzyingly painful. From time to time I would be released and then the whole exercise was repeated again. I wanted to cry out but I was conscious that my cry should be brave and not cowardly. When I heard my first cry, I was not disappointed. It was like a bull's angry bellow. Anyone would have recognized it as the cry of a warrior. I only cried out when the pain was truly unbearable; I tried my best to remain silent as far as I could. When they raised me from the cot I clenched my teeth hard and stared at them. I always had the habit of grinding my teeth and now, in the throes of being tortured, the tendency became even more pronounced.

I was again taken out and seated on the stool in front of the DSP. He said, 'When we capture big gangsters they surrender in front of us.'

I replied, 'We are not gangsters, we are patriots.'

He said, 'We could break Chetan in seven days and we will break this one in a matter of a few more days.'

I snorted in contempt. He did not write anything on the paper and took the empty sheets with him. He never interrogated me again. Comrade Vaid was watching all this helplessly.

After the DSP had left I was tortured with an iron rod which they called 'kilometre'. The four-inch-thick rod was a yard and a quarter long and it was placed under my knees. Then a strong policeman would use all his might to double up my legs by placing pressure on my waist. In this process, my backbone would scrape the floor and get bruised. I was taken out and told that all my companions had been arrested and that they had revealed everything under torture. They wanted me to accompany them to arrest some other comrades. The police wanted to stamp out the Naxalites once and for all. They knew where everyone was but they wanted one comrade to accompany them while they were arresting another so that his morale was broken. This was being done so that they could later launch a negative propaganda campaign that we were betraying those people who had given us food and shelter.

There was Comrade Vaid sitting in front of me while I was wondering whether he had betrayed me to the police. If he had, it was something to be ashamed of. I was told that Comrade Chetan, who had been captured before I was, had revealed everything about me. But where was he now? The police even knew details about my personal life, and they used these to torment me further. They also knew about Comrade Chetan's daughter, and this worried me greatly. I feared for her life. I thought, 'That girl must be saved at all costs.'

This mental torture was worse than physical torture. They were trying to diminish my revolutionary zeal. However, they did not drag this on for too long.

— ❦ —

Looking back, I believe it is possible that Comrade Vaid had given the police all the information. But then, perhaps they were just using Comrade Chetan's name to weaken my resolve.

That was a time the comrades showed their ugliest side. There were rumours of many of them betraying each other to the police. But I had still not given up my faith in them, because I felt they must be faithful to the party and would not stoop so low.

At that time I had no idea that there were intelligence agents among our party cadre. Much later, after being released from prison, I used the term 'CIA' for Vairagi. Others were quick to correct me, 'He was not a CIA but a KGB agent.' This was what led me to understand Vairagi, the great betrayer. Still, I could never be quite sure who his accomplices had been.

— ❦ —

I don't know why but I could not sit still in the interrogation centre. Often the policemen would keep me standing all night to torture me. The reason for my insomnia could have been that the police had fed me some tablets. I refused food for some time, but then I gave in and started eating because I desperately needed some strength to face the torture. When I had first refused food, one policeman said, 'He is very clever.' I did not like this because I hate cleverness. Also, I feel that not eating food is a sympathy-gaining trick. But maybe I was restless because the police seemed to know everything about my ill-fated love life. They told me they knew me well because they had been hearing me recite my poems at different symposia. Just look at the irony that these erstwhile admirers of my poetry could offer me only beatings and torture.

I was an atheist, but before sunrise and sunset, my hands would come together. In one such moment one young, lanky, clean-shaven constable came up to me. He twisted his waist like a eunuch and, swinging his hands, he hit me on my ear. My ear hurt and itched and after a while I could no longer hear from it. The boy tried to talk about my romances but I kept quiet. He then said, 'We will see to it that worms crawl all over your body.' I was reminded of my poem 'Hijarhe' (Eunuchs): *'Jeharhe gaonde ne pyar oh galat gaonde ne'* (Those who sing of love sing wrong). The mention of worms brought Shiv Kumar to my mind. However, a new development distracted me. I gathered from the conversation of the policemen that someone had just been captured. But I could not be sure. The policemen often played tricks, sometimes pretending to interrogate or torture a captive in the adjoining room so that I would be frightened into losing my resolve. In another room one would question the other and it would seem that they were interrogating somebody.

The next day, one police officer got hold of me early in the morning and he kept talking to me inside a room. He was a Sikh and his beard was grey. He seemed to have come from outside. He told me, 'We believe that you are a patriot but your other companions are very dirty men. You are our son.' There was one constable who belonged to a lower caste. He used to sit quietly by my side, holding the handcuffs during the torture. I could see the anger in his eyes at the way I was being tortured. At the Sikh's comment he got up and, putting the 'kilometre' by the wall, went out.

It was the month of May and the sun was harsh. I was reminded of a line from one of my poems: '*Suraj da suhah gola hor vadda hor uchcha uthiya*' (The red ball of the sun grew larger and rose higher into the sky). Uniforms and belts were hanging inside the room. A few policemen came in. I was again made to lie down on my stomach. The handcuff was pulled forward, my hair was held tightly and a heavy iron weight was placed under my knees. I was subjected to the same old pattern of torment with the 'kilometre', after which I was taken to the DSP's office. The hot sand beneath my feet and the fiery sun above indicated that it was midday.

Pannu was bent over his table and looked somewhat like a schoolmaster pouring over the attendance register. He looked up and said, 'Take him with you.'

I tried to move forward but my legs were stiff and aching. It was as though my flesh had been roasted.

Pannu spoke again, 'Do you know where we are sending you? You will now help us in raiding the hiding places of your comrades.'

I was in such mental and physical agony that nothing seemed to register. All I could think of was getting my hands on a weapon of some sort. If there was a police rifle lying around, I could still try to use it by pressing the trigger with my foot. There was no way I was going to betray my comrades. I would much rather end my own life.

I was lifted and placed in a jeep and all the policemen crowded in. I asked them if I could lie down on the floor of the jeep to straighten my back; they agreed. I immediately did so, pushing my head under the front seat. Faced with no other choice, I tried to strangle myself with my turban. The policemen heard my choking and they stopped the jeep. My body was fighting to breathe. I felt happy that I had been able to convey to them that I would not betray any comrade. They lifted

me up and said, 'What are you doing? We thought you
are very brave!' I did not have anything to say and they
put me back on the seat.

No remand had been taken. Comrade Bujha Singh
used to say that if the police continued with torture,
it was best to start hitting your head on the floor.
I was not very convinced of this because the police
were habitually killing whomever they deemed to
be criminals and then discarding the bodies. So they
would not be moved by anyone banging his head on
the floor. They could even disgrace the women of
the revolutionary's family. They would catch hold of
other members of the family and put them through
torture. The touts had scared the families of the boys
who were underground, so much so that the families
had turned into slaves of sorts. Many would curse their
sons and even wish for their death so that they would
be free from police harassment. It was said that the
left parties like the CPI and the CPM were aiding the
police. Littérateurs had also succumbed to some kind
of a false peace.

I was dropped by the policemen at the Ropar police
station. The station house officer (SHO), who had
pockmarks on his face, made me sit in a side room.
A slim policeman was sitting there, cane in hand, and
two others were lounging around. These policemen

seemed to be more human than those in the special squad whom I had just encountered. I kept staring at the wall, wishing that I could jump over it and run to my freedom. Just then the havaldar started asking me gently why we were resorting to violence.

I quoted from the Gurbani and said, '*Papan bajon hove nahi.*' (Wealth is not amassed without sins.)

As if in response, the havaldar recited the second line, '*Moyan saath na jaaye.*' (Wealth does not go with you to the next world.)

He did not say anything after this. In fact, I asked him if his name was Harjit Singh. He replied with a sad smile, 'No, I do not have such a beautiful name.'

The policemen who had left me here had probably informed my new custodian about how Pannu had been nonplussed because of me, and perhaps this was why I was not being questioned. As they left, I saw them talking to the policemen from Ropar. In the evening I was taken in a police van to the senior superintendent of police (SSP). The SSP, who was a relative of the maharaja of Patiala, spoke to me politely. He offered me water and also drank a glass himself. He instructed the policemen on what I should be asked further.

I was asked to sit down on a cot which had a sack spread on it. I felt relieved for the first time although the earth seemed to be spinning like a potter's wheel. This was a moment of respite but a young policeman who was tipsy came and sat next to me. He started pulling at my hair.

I screamed out, 'If you trouble me like this, I will kill myself!'

The policeman shouted loudly, 'Just hear what this bloke is saying. He is threatening to commit suicide.' He then turned to me and said, 'We will drain off your blood and throw you in the canal.'

I then heard the thanedar shout, 'No one is to talk to him! If I see anyone doing so, I will fix him.'

After the thanedar left, a telephone call at the police station reported a quarrel in the city. The constables went there and returned with a man. When they asked him to lie down he started shouting, '*Waheguru! Waheguru!*' He was given a blow with the lathi and sent home. I was reminded of the well-off blacksmith family of Samrala who would scare their servants and employees by saying, 'Should we call up number eight?' At times just saying number eight was enough. I did not have to look into the directory to know that it was the telephone number of Samrala police station.

My handcuffs were removed and I was put in the lock-up close to the gate. There was soft moonlight outside my cell and a terrible stink inside. On one side there was a heap of straw mats and one mat had been spread out on the floor. As I sat down on the mat, I realized that it was soaking wet and infested with bugs. In another corner, which was dark, an earthen pitcher had been placed. The stench was so bad that I found it difficult to sleep. When the lock-up door was opened, I was already awake. I was taken out. Two stout Sikh constables as well as a few short ones were there to receive me. One of them slapped his hand on my shoulder and said, 'When a goat is taken to the butcher, it comes to know what its fate will be!'

I was bundled into a jeep and it started moving far away from the city into the wilderness. We stopped by a grove of tall mango trees and many thorny bushes. I could also see some houses. I got out and was trying walk properly in spite of the stiffness and pain in my legs. I heard someone shout from the mango grove, 'Just see how he walks! Teach him to walk properly.'

Two policemen were seated there with a table between them. I was taken to a quarter. There were two rooms adjoining the courtyard that I had entered. There was a tree near the urinals on one side, while a dirty, stinking mattress was lying in the centre of the courtyard. In one corner, I saw a thick, wooden stick.

The constables surrounded me and one of them said, 'Do you know I am from the Amritsar inquiry centre!'

My handcuffs were removed and my arms were tied behind my back. One constable standing behind me pulled my hair and, slamming his knee into my back, made me sit down. Two constables rushed to catch hold of my legs, while two more held me by my upper arms. My hair was pulled down and my neck bent backwards. They pulled my legs in opposite directions till the legs could not be stretched any further. But the policeman behind me said, 'One inch more.' At this my legs were jerked. I was beside myself with pain.

He again shouted, 'One inch more.' And they held me tight in that position saying that they did not want to question me any further.

As they were taking me towards the door, I saw a young thanedar standing there. He came to me and slapped me hard. I came out of the door and was trying to balance my body when the inspector shouted, 'Just see how he walks; break his leg.' They took me inside and subjected my legs to the same torture with renewed zeal. They brought me back again and I was given a heavy blow with a stick on the back of my leg. Words cannot describe the pain I felt. I had to limp a few steps when the constables pushed me to the ground and I sat down. They implied that I should bow my head and wish the inspector. But the inspector did not say anything.

An old policeman was sitting next to me and he started talking to me. I learnt from him that the doctor from Khamano had been captured. He was beaten up so badly that he had lost his mind. The police played a cruel game with him. They told him that his young girls had been brought to the police station and were being dishonoured in another room. Hearing this, the doctor started raving and ranting like a madman and shouted all night.

The police did not allow me to rest at night and in the morning I was interrogated again. After that I was put under the supervision of a constable. At night I was asked to sleep somewhere else. The next day and night passed peacefully. In the morning I was taken out to where some jeeps were waiting along with several police officers in plain clothes.

The jeeps took us past the canal and we reached the quarters. I was not allowed to look outside but I felt that it was a caravan of three or four jeeps. The inspector told the others, 'We will not take him any further.' I was taken inside the quarters and tied to a cot. I saw the BSF inspector's son standing there. He was one of the three who had entered the Chamkaur Sahib police station during the action. He had come to see me a few days before the police had caught me and, as per Vairagi's instructions, had even taken my pistol away from me. I had been fond of him. Whenever we met we would talk to each other but Vairagi would be quick to separate us. He was one of Vairagi's special fellows and was always armed. Even before the attack at Chamkaur Sahib, the pistol was taken away from me and given to him because we were thirteen and had only twelve firearms. I was left without even a stick to defend myself.

Come to think of it, Vairagi never did like me very much. One day, Vairagi was criticizing Comrade Chetan and was quoting Mao Tse-tung. I had the gall to ask, 'To which year does this quotation date back?'

Irritated, Vairagi had retorted, 'Never you mind! We will fix you.'

At this police station, the difference between the special staff and the non-special staff was quite apparent. The ranks were clearly divided on caste lines. This had always been so but here it was more prominent. One section of the police was special and the other non-special. The ordinary policemen were made to feel irresponsible or incompetent. The policemen here were more congenial and I was more at ease with them.

Once, I jokingly told the havaldar, 'No matter what you say, the police will be the police.'

At this the havaldar responded with a laugh, 'And comrades will be comrades.' This havaldar's face was dimpled. He reminded me of the girl whose mother had thrown the tumbler, from which I had drank tea, into the fire to purify it.

This police station was new and had come into existence only recently after Ropar had been made a district. The Congress was in power. At that time, I did not know that the Congress had built this police station after coming to power. The police were made of members from different castes. Inspector Pritam Singh here was a Nai (barber) by caste whereas the special staff comprised only Jats and Brahmins. Some policemen at Ropar would even take out their gutkha and do paath or say their prayers. The second time when I was brought here, Inspector Pritam Singh had shouted loudly and told everyone that I should be tortured mercilessly.

However, I was treated relatively better here. No

one asked me my name or the name of my village. In fact, they all knew it well. I was surprised when a middle-aged policeman revealed in conversation that my mother's name was Chinti. He also said that my home was on the temple road.

At times I felt that I was actually being treated like a human being. One day, when it was raining outside and I was alone, I was urinating. Inspector Pritam Singh was passing by and he immediately went the other way so I would not be embarrassed. Another time, I was made to lie down on a table and my handcuffs were tied to one of the table's legs. Seeing this arrangement, Pritam Singh said, 'Why have you done this? One day he will run away carrying the table on his head.'

During the last few days there, when they were bringing me back from the court, the jeep nearly met with an accident but the driver was smart and he managed to avert a head-on collision.

My old comrade, the son of the BSF officer, had given the police a lot of information. As for me, I finally accepted the case of the revolver that they had slapped on me because I felt they would only humiliate me further if I didn't. Even worse, they might bring members of my family to the quarters and torture them in front of me.

The next morning, I was handcuffed and taken out. I felt what a circus lion feels after being let out of the cage. I looked at my hair in my own shadow and it seemed to resemble a lion's mane. It was unwashed and thick with dried blood, and I was aware of the stench rising from it.

All these days I even had to empty my bowels in someone else's presence and this was another kind of torture.

That day the policemen thrashed me well. I noticed that one policeman had blood on his beard. My pyjamas, with their thin maroon stripes, were taken off me and thrown aside. My thick, dark-blue kurta had absorbed the blood and no stains were visible. They were saying, 'Give him the lambardar treatment.' The 'lambardar' was a wooden version of the 'kilometre'. But when they saw that my legs were badly bruised they dropped the idea and started stretching my legs instead. I felt helpless and mentally unhinged. They pushed me in that condition in front of Inspector Pritam Singh. This was the worst kind of punishment because I had not been disrobed before this. In shame, I knelt down on one knee before the inspector. The thought struck me that this scene was reminiscent of Hanuman kneeling before Ram and Sita. The BSF officer was also there and was glaring at me.

They interrogated me again about the Chamkaur attack. The police had decided to implicate me in this case well and proper. The son of the BSF officer had become an informer on the promise that he would be set free. I had not told any lies to the police and it was plain to see that I was unarmed and a poet. I would have been let off but they did not want to do that. Besides this case, they were implicating me in other cases too.

'We need more cases. Otherwise this new centre may be dismantled.' That's what the policemen often said. And needless to say, an endless series of arrests and brutalities followed. One day, the police caught hold of a thief who, with his unkempt beard, even looked the role. He was tied up next to me. Waving his cane, a constable threatened him, 'You rascal, we will throw you in the hospital and inject you with poison.' But he was taken to the lock-up in the evening and the interrogation was done there. He was also given one day's remand. So, a thief enjoyed greater privileges than the likes of me.

Another day, a man was brought to the police station. He was given a few blows with a stick and these were enough to get him to confess. He told the policemen where he had kept the gun. He also gave them the name of the man who had hired him for the murder. When the policemen tried to remove his clothes, he resisted. At this, he was given another blow and paraded naked in the courtyard. This man, a self-confessed murderer, was trembling with fear. Finally, he was allowed to wear his clothes. He was sitting close to me. His handcuffs were tied to the bars. Later, he turned to me saying he wanted to urinate but there was no policeman around to unlock the handcuffs. I told him to urinate in his shoe, then throw the urine out. And that is what he did. I had learnt to cope with the absurdities and hardships of life in the lock-up.

Following that, the police brought in a boy

implicated in a revolver case. He was beaten so badly that he took them to search his house. On another occasion, they brought an old man and his two sons. They were camel-riders and very tall. The police made them do sit-ups; then one constable pointed towards me and said, 'Do you want to be treated like him?' At this, all three of them folded their hands and started pleading, 'Please don't treat us like him. Don't beat us.' Only then did I realize how frightful I looked—a glance at me was enough to scare anyone.

My interrogations also continued amidst all this. I would often hear these familiar words from the mouth of a new policeman, 'So you bloody Chamars, you want our land?' And the brutalities would follow.

After subjecting me to torture, a policeman would turn me upside down and give my legs a rub-down of sorts so that the traces of the torture would not show. It was then that I decided to follow the advice given by Bujha Singh of hitting the ground with my head. Earlier, I had thought that this was something demeaning but now I was forced to resort to it. When I hit the ground three or four times, the policemen lifted me and said, 'This is something new, something new.'

They took me to the inspector who said, 'We want the revolver that was with you.' And he banged the table with his hand.

I said firmly, 'I have no revolver.'

That night one thanedar sat all night with me talking about the revolver that never was.

To seek respite from my life in the lock-up, my mind started turning towards poetry. The rains were just about to start.

I was still hopeful that even though our revolutionary group had been crushed, it would one day rise again. It was evident that the police did not want to let go of me. However, I had made up my mind that even though they had implicated me in a false case, accusing me of possessing a revolver, I would deny the charges in court and say that I had nothing to do with any revolver of any kind.

But that was before the endless drill of torture had sapped my spirit completely.

One day, dense clouds suddenly appeared in the sky and it started raining. I was sitting alone in the veranda. The police were very happy that I had accepted the false charge in the revolver case; and I was happy that I would be rid of them.

On the first day of the trial, they took me to be presented in court, but then brought me away. I spent the night in a lock-up at Kharar.

The next day, the judge asked me, 'Do you have anything to say?'

I said, 'No.'

A few years of rigorous imprisonment and three hundred rupees as fine. This was very little by way of punishment in comparison to the torture that I had been subjected to by then. And I was eager to be released from the special squad's barbarism. It is true that one was also beaten up while serving a regular jail sentence, but the brutalities would not be so severe.

'You are just like us, you rascal! You are a bit fiery, we are a bit calm.'

'We do care for a good man.'

'For God's sake, give up this party and we will support you.'

Such were the words uttered by the policemen there.

Now that I was being taken to be presented in court, I was given a bath for the first time. It had been several weeks since I'd been brought here. I was even wearing the same clothes. I was scrubbing my clothes during the bath when a fat policeman approached me. I think he was a Brahmin because he had once hit me with a stick and taunted, 'So you Chamars want land!' Now, as I was rinsing my kurta, he said to me, 'When your party comes into power, we will be with you.'

When the policemen were taking me to Ropar and we were sitting at a dhaba, I asked, 'So now you will be rid of me?'

At this the fat fellow said, 'Do we have to tear open our hearts to convince you that we have no hatred for you?'

I was put in one long room in the jail. My companion in the room was that boy, Lakhwinder, who had been left behind in the Chamkaur Sahib police station. He was so happy to see me that he started clapping. He specially arranged for some milk for me and introduced me to the others. Then he lay down and said, 'Put your head on my chest and recite that poem which I had heard from you by the side of the canal.' I tried to think but the poem that he wanted to hear—in which the word 'revolution' was repeated several times—was written by someone else.

Lakhwinder told me that he had heard from the people who had seen me in the interrogation centre that I had been horrifically tortured. A straightforward boy, he told me his own story too. He thought being given a jail term was ultimately for the better.

After some time, I was moved to the central jail at Patiala. Lakhwinder was still in the Ropar jail. During my stay there I had been able to convince Lakhwinder that the police and the judiciary were hand in glove. It had already been a month since I was brought to the jail but I had not been presented in court again.

Prisoners are strange beings. Sometimes they start singing, and sometimes they will be ready for a brawl. However, other prisoners gave us a somewhat reverential treatment. I learnt from experience that the supervisors in the jail were put off with me because the ordinary prisoners would give me their rations, etc., for safekeeping; otherwise the supervisors would keep the best for themselves and distribute the leftovers to the prisoners.

One day a supervisor told me, 'This is good jaggery, so keep it safe with you.'

I asked, 'Why don't you distribute it?'

The supervisor was playing cards at that time. He left his game and came to hit me with a stick. I too stood up and he retreated.

I was presented before the superintendent, Bachan Singh, who said, 'Will you stop your party propaganda or not?'

I was puzzled and could not understand the connection of this incident with the party or its propaganda. However, I was moved to the enclosed portion of the jail where dangerous prisoners were kept. Some of the prisoners here were mad and others quarrelsome, and there were some others who had revolted against the practices in the jail. There were two supervisors, but one of them had been literally driven out of the jail by the inmates—he had escaped aboard a truck carrying wheat stolen from the jail.

I never politely greeted any official in the jail but the supervisor did not admonish me for this impertinence whereas he would thrash others who behaved thus. The reason for this was that the jail doctor had declared me 'mental' and so the supervisor did not bother me much. While I was in there, Gursharan Singh came with his whole family to stage plays for the prisoners. I signed a note with my good wishes and sent it to him. I would do rigorous work in the prison without any shame or complaint because I now considered myself a volunteer of the comrades.

One day I asked the supervisor the height of the wall of the enclosure where the prisoners were taken to do farm work. He laughed and said, 'Just as much as your height!' I looked up at him questioningly, and he said, 'Yes.' He also conveyed to me that I would not be taken out for farm work.

One havaldar took a great dislike towards me and started troubling me. Every other day he would search my belongings. I had a quarter of a pencil with me but he seized it. I had kept some surma as well. I would write with it on the wall, and then transfer it on to a piece of paper before hiding it in my shoe.

I recall another incident around the festival of Diwali. I came across a photograph in the newspaper. It was a picture of Indira Gandhi and I was quite mesmerized by it. She was standing in a victorious pose which was similar to that of Stalin's in a portrait I had earlier seen printed in his biography. I was not able to take my eyes off her portrait.

On Diwali night the supervisor placed a little lamp under the mango tree close to the room where I used to grind wheat every day. This festive gesture reminded me of the world outside the prison and that night I wrote on the wall, with a piece of coal, my poem 'Diwali di Raat': . . .

The newspaper did not carry any news about

Naxalbari. Most of the prisoners were a religious lot and would engage in path puja and such rituals. I too had created some rituals for myself. I had saved a datun stick and had cut out a rectangle of cloth from my quilt. At night, after the grinding room was shut down, I would fix the datun stick in the lid of the Tinopal container and raise the flag.

One day my family came to see me. My younger brother's eyes were full of tears. The next time my mother came alone. She had brought some food for me. After some time she got up to leave. As she was leaving, I picked up the things she had brought and, instead of retreating inside, I started following her. The jail officials caught hold of me and I was hastily locked in a cell.

The older prisoners would look for a chance to oil their moustaches and go for a stroll to the other side of the prison where young inmates were kept. In this unhappy environment, I would look happily at the woman warden who seemed so fragile and beautiful. But other prisoners told me that she was a horrible woman. Rumour had it that her husband had knifed her and then he had committed suicide.

Freedom

What does one call those words?
Words that walk like sighs
Scared, the birds
start singing all of a sudden . . .

After I was released from prison, I really did not know
where to go. Strolling about, I reached the bus stand
and decided to head home. I had got the barber to cut
my hair very short, so when I reached my village no
one seemed to recognize me.

While I was home, the son of a communist activist
brought me a note with Harbhajan Halwarvi's address
scrawled on it and asked me to go and look him up. I
had gone to see Halwarvi a few days earlier but he had
not been home. I left him a note. I then found that I
did not have money to pay the bus fare back to my
village, so I borrowed a rupee from a boy in Halwarvi's
neighbourhood and returned home.

Now when I went to see him a second time, I learnt
that a thanedar had been killed by some smugglers

outside Halwarvi's house. There were police all around. I went to that boy to return him his rupee and he nervously mumbled that I should run away from there because the police were looking for me. I thought that my note to Halwarvi had probably been found by the police. When I reached Samrala, I learnt that my house had been raided. I did not know where to go. I just started roaming around looking for shelter. No friend or relative was willing to help me. I fled to Dadi's village, but the possibility of a police retaliation made them very afraid so they asked me to leave.

Finally I went to a comrade who worked as a full-timer for the Communist Party of India (Marxist). I told him the whole story and he said, 'It is the case of the murder of a police officer. Who is guilty and who is not will be decided much later but the police will thrash any suspect they get hold of.'

He gave me money to reach Khanna and I left the place. Since Chamkaur was close to this area, policemen were travelling in buses. So I decided it would be safer to walk through the nearby fields. For a long time I walked and ran through those fields; then I reached a road. Crossing it, I asked a man sitting there how far the nearest railway station was. He told me that it was three kilometres away. Following the railway track, I reached the station and boarded a train headed for Gobindgarh.

By and large, I received no help wherever I went. But the next day, when I went to the college in Gobindgarh, one boy there gave me fifteen rupees. With limited options, I realized that there was no way out but to go away to the safety of Uttar Pradesh (UP). When the police were unable to get me to name anyone, they started terrorizing my family and friends. Even the poets were too scared to help me. I was thus left to my own devices.

While I was roaming around in UP, five rupees were snatched from my pocket. I knew I couldn't go on like this, wandering aimlessly. I remembered a farm, owned by a kind-hearted Punjabi, that I had visited in the past. I decided to go there. Subsequently, I met a man from Amritsar who was carrying some grain on his head. He sold that grain and gave me three rupees and fifty paise. Thanking him, I walked all the way to reach Milani.

When I was about to board the train there, I met two friendly people who offered me a seat in the coach right behind the engine. There were many policemen stationed at both the Shahjahan station and the Milani station. I gathered that these two men were from the police. They offered me a bidi, and I noticed how they would glance meaningfully at each other while engaging me in conversation. The train stopped at Gola station and one of them moved out of the coach. I too went and sat in another coach which was teeming with UP locals. But I still felt uneasy—and so my instincts took over. I tore the newspaper in my hand and threw it away. I also tied my thin, grey muslin turban—which was still wet from having been recently washed—around my head.

But I saw that there were a number of policemen in this coach too, including a Sikh who was wearing glasses. I passed them and went to the other side but as soon as I lit my bidi, I saw a group of policemen rushing towards the train. I hid the bidi in my fist, leapt out of the train and, crossing the tracks, hid myself. A long time later, I quietly moved into the tracts of recently irrigated paddy fields. The paddy was waist-high; at some places the water in the fields came up to my ankles and at others it was even deeper. I kept walking from one field to the next till I reached my destination.

Despite the inky darkness, I recognized the road and the orchard at once because, some ten years ago, I used to come here to deliver sugar cane. It was then that I became familiar with this orchard. After walking a little distance I left the road and stepped into the fields. On the way, I came across a drain. A thorn pierced my foot as I stepped in it. The drain was neither deep nor wide. At a distance I could hear some people talking. I called out, '*Arrey bhaiya!*'

No one answered my call. I started shouting loudly but there was still no response. I saw a machan in the fields and I climbed it. It was as wide and long as a good-sized bed. I put aside my trousers which I was carrying rolled up under my arm. I took off my shirt too and draped myself with my turban, which was now nearly dry, and lay down.

I was able to sleep in fits and starts. In the morning, I saw the rays of the sun and a man standing close by. He was staring at the machan and a teenage boy was standing next to him. I said, '*Arrey bhaiya*, I called out so many times last night but got no answer. What if someone was dying? You would still not have come out?'

He said, 'We thought some dacoit had come into the fields.'

I said, 'All right, now give me a bidi. I so wanted to smoke last night.' After smoking the bidi, I asked him, 'How far is the village?'

He replied, 'It is very close. You will not have to walk much.'

Now this was really amazing. I had come to the right place in the dark night. It was the same village from where one turned to go to the farm where I was headed. It was hardly five kilometres away. I went to the road and had a cup of tea with the little money left with me and also bought a bundle of bidis and a matchbox. It was still morning when I set out, and the path went through the woods. I reached the farm around noon. I was a mess—hungry, tired, dirty. There were leeches clinging to my legs. As I washed up at the tap, pulling away the leeches, I saw blood trickling down my legs.

I had stayed at this farm earlier and knew the owner who had a big bookshop in Ludhiana. I used to buy books from his shop. He wanted a farmhand for this piece of land that he had bought here. Someone suggested my name and he hired me for thirty rupees a month. I had thought that I would simply be overseeing the place and would have time to read and write. However, on reaching there I had found that I would have to do hard manual labour. Disappointed, I had returned home.

Now I was there at his farm again. The owner was happy to see me. He told me that since he was going back to Punjab to be with his wife, who was expecting a baby, he would leave me at the farm to mark the attendance of the workers. This worked out perfectly for me.

He returned with his family after a month and a half. One day he told me that Harbans Lal, my friend and comrade from the old days, wanted to meet me. Harbans had moved to these parts in fear of being caught as a Naxalite. I was not keen to go to him but felt compelled to do so since I was no longer needed at the farm. Harbans had set up a shop to repair electric motors and he was quite friendly with the local policemen. I reached his house and met his wife too. She was as thin as he was fat.

I wondered if I should also learn to repair electric motors and work with Harbans. This job might be more lucrative than farm work. So Harbans kept me at his shop in Palia while he stayed with his family a few miles away. After some days, he told me that I was not able to learn the work, so he suggested that I go to his aunt's farm instead. I went there and laboured hard for more than a year. Harbans would claim wages on my behalf and also drink liquor whereas I got only two meals a day from this poor farmer family.

One day he took me back to Palia and sent me off with another man. My new job involved taking this man's cattle out to graze and also teaching his children. This man had a collection of books and he was appreciative of my interest in reading and writing. He became quite fond of me. This was one place where I felt comfortable and found the environment conducive to literary work. Here I got the opportunity to read a Hindi translation of Nehru's *The Discovery of India* and enjoyed it a lot. Long ago I had written the poem 'Athan' (Evening Tide) in which I had obliquely referred to India before the coming of the Aryans. I wrote a number of poems while at that place which were later published in *Bahut Saare Suraj* (A Million Suns). But soon this idyll was lost.

Harbans came to me one day and said, 'I will take you back with me and we will set up a new shop. I know a boy whose family has one shop on Lucknow's Lotus Road and one at Lakhimpur. We will join them and you will be able to learn the motor-winding work better.'

He brought me back to Palia. I learnt that his family had gone to Punjab and his work had come to a standstill. After some days, we went via Gonda to Lakhimpur. His friend Sharif was at the shop there. A good-hearted fellow, he was nicely dressed in Lucknavi clothes and his manner was cultured. Sharif and Harbans would go out for work while Sharif's younger brother, Hamza, and few other boys learnt the job. I joined them. I went to the shop very regularly.

—◆—

After my days in jail, much had changed for me. Earlier, life had seemed to be an imprisonment of sorts but the days in prison had been so distressing that the world outside seemed beautiful. I experienced a new joy in simple things like watching the effigies of Ravana burn during Dussehra. I would even delight in going for a ride on the merry-go-round which had been set up as part of the festivities. Incidentally, the festival celebrations would continue here for a full month: shops would be set up at fairs; there would be folk performances and poetry symposia. I was enjoying every moment of it.

I also participated in a poetry symposium. Here I heard a woman poet, whose soft back was touching my shoulder, recite a poem on Gautam Buddha:

If you had to go, you had to go
but at least you could have bid me adieu.

I also heard some poems recited in praise of Indira Gandhi. One old man shook his head sorrowfully because that was a time when the battle for Bangladesh had been won. I had prepared a ghazal for the occasion. When my name was announced, I ran up to the stage and read out a ghazal in Punjabi. The Hindu boys did not want to hear it. Later I scolded the boys who were hooting at me. The boys at the shop were very impressed with the fact that I was a poet and they started taking an interest in me. A neighbouring shopkeeper called Vajpai also joined in the conversation and recited a long epic that he had written on Bangladesh.

———

As time went by, I could see that Sharif and Hamza were very pleased with my sincerity and hard work at the shop. They had gone home to Lucknow to settle things for the marriage of their sister to a young man studying in Lakhimpur. He would come to see me nearly every day and recite his ghazals for my benefit.

I was taken to Lucknow for the marriage and was in charge of pitching the tent in addition to other duties. I did my work well and Sharif's mother kept me there. Around ten in the morning, I would take the food to the shop and return home with the others in the evening. The poet Aftab Lucknavi lived nearby and he would receive me very fondly because I was a poet.

During my stay there, the city was ravaged by floods. A large portion of the Imambara—one of the grand shrines that was such an attraction in Lucknow, particularly renowned for the labyrinth in its midst—

was under water. A circus lion, besieged by the rising
water level, had managed to escape by jumping over
the wall. Grain was being gathered for the flood victims
and I was given the job of weighing it out.

After the floods subsided, the roads opened and
I returned to Lakhimpur with Hamza. Harbans
suggested that we should go to Mohammadi where he
wanted to learn more about motor repair. We reached
the farm of Lachhman Singh. A rather unhappy man,
he was rankled by the fact that he had no children and
was very upset because his brother-in-law wanted to
grab his land. Harbans and Lachhman would go to the
shop and I would work on the farm.

This farm was nearly fifteen to sixteen acres in area.
There were four villages, almost equidistant from the
farm, located in four different directions.

On the east was the village of Sisiar which was
inhabited by Jhaura and Pasia people. Thakurs, of
course, were in majority there and they were a real
terror. They would loot the harvested crops, destroy
the cattle and pick fights every other day. While I was
there, they started plundering the field of Sumedh
Chamar who had been rented out a piece of land by
Lachhman. Lachhman's nephew tried to stop them but
in vain. There was mayhem in the fields. The Thakurs
were all over the place. I stopped one of them and said,
'You have plundered his crop but do not think that
you have frightened us. Have some shame . . . some
shame.' Saying this, I retreated.

The village towards the north, called Chak Wakarpur, was not very old. Almost all the homes belonged to one clan. The eldest brother was called the lambardar (headman). Three brothers tilled the land and one worked as a driver. This was a clan of Pathans who looked like the Choorhas of Punjab. There was only one home in Chak Wakarpur that was peopled by Chamars.

There was a home in the Purail village, towards the west, that belonged to a Sayeed who treated me like a son. This village had families of different castes but the Thakurs ruled the roost.

The fourth village was called Kuraili and was dominated by the Chamars although the landlords too had one home there.

Life went on at a steady, predictable pace. One day something wonderful happened—I received a book of my poems. These had been published by Prem Prakash in my absence and he had sent me five copies. Later Prem Prakash and I exchanged a few letters.

Harbans had gone away. Lachhman had taken his wife and adopted nephew with him and they were now living in Mohammadi. He had left me behind to supervise the farm, as one would leave a brother.

In Search of a Kinder God

How sweet are these words
dedicated to God.
I wish my last words
would be:
'I have complete faith in you!'
I want to steal this line
and dedicate it to the Revolution.

The next year the farm was rented out to Muslims. The three partners were Mistri Rahim Bakhsh, Bashir Ahmad and Wali. On the first day they arrived, one of them stretched out on my bed and the two others sat next to me by the store. They started addressing me as Gianiji. Lachhman had told them about me. Now my duty was to start the motor and keep the accounts.

Girls would come to work on the farm. They were from the lower-caste families of the village to the south. The girls and the boys who worked on the farm would often engage in fun and frolic. The girls wore medium-priced saris of bright colours and they looked like butterflies in the field. The three girls who came regularly were Ram Beni, Maya Devi and Mainiya. Three boys accompanied them. Sometimes they would make one of the girls sit on a bamboo and lift her up as though they were carrying her in a palanquin. I told them that they should not do so, but they did not pay any heed. Sometimes Bashir or his partners would flirt with these girls.

One day Bashir started singing a song, *Kajra lagake, bindiya sajake, jayio na* (Do not step out with kohl-lined eyes and vermilion on your forehead). I interpreted this song as a warning to his wives about the rampant exploitation at the hands of landlords. He was warning them that they should not venture out all dressed up and beautiful. Bashir would often sing a bhajan in his sonorous voice: *Chaar jane mujhe le ke chale, Ganga ki dhunden dagariya chalat beria* (Four pall-bearers carry me as they walk, looking for the way to the Ganga River). Rahim Bakhsh was also fond of listening to and reciting poetry. I had completed my manuscript of *Bahut Saare Suraj* by then and all the poems included in it were written on the farm.

I was chopping vegetables one day when one of the girls came and tried to act familiar with me. I said, 'How dare you, Ram Beni! I will scoop out your eyes with my chopping knife.' At this, Bashir and the others, who were standing at a little distance, started laughing. This was the day I realized that something within me had fundamentally changed. In fact, I had been noticing for some time that I had become very irritable. I could no longer bear any sort of loud noise, even the rousing beat of a drum. If music was played I would cover my ears with a cloth because the songs disturbed my thoughts and writings.

Nonetheless, I was disturbed that I had scolded a girl who was merely trying to be friendly with me. So I started making a conscious effort to overcome my shyness and inhibition. To live shackled by a disturbed mind was yet another sort of imprisonment, perhaps the worst kind. One evening I thought to myself that I had been treated all my life like a dog. So be it! I actually started barking and prancing about like a dog.

But slowly I tried to move towards some kind of a normalcy. I started listening to music on the transistor.

—∞—

The people around were quite kind and friendly. I had never abandoned the farm even when the Thakurs of Sisiar village went about plundering the fields. Like I said before, I did not hesitate tell one of the Thakurs that we were not frightened of them. The news of my bravery must have reached the surrounding villages. If I did not go to the Muslim lambardar, he would come and talk to me. One day, he was discussing some medicine with me and Lachhman's querulous mother too was there. The lambardar said, 'If you are looking for a doctor, go to a Muslim; and if you are looking for a lawyer, go to a Hindu.' He added that Hindus were very good at telling lies to win a case. At this Lachhman's mother said, 'True, a Hindu thrives on lies and a Musalman on shared bread.'

The boys of Chak Wakarpur were particularly fond of me and they would often want to know things about the Guru Granth Sahib, taking me to be a warrior of sorts from Punjab. In the mornings and evenings I would go to this village to fetch milk. There was no purdah in the Hindu families. In any case, a low-caste man is hardly considered someone who can pose any danger to a woman of an upper-caste home. But one day I had a different experience. It was drizzling so I walked into the courtyard of the lambardar's home. Almost instantly, the lambardar's brother pushed me out because the women were sitting there without purdah. I was happy because, for the first time, I had been treated like a man. The Muslim women would talk from behind the curtain, and they had made small peepholes in the doors to see what was going on outside.

One day Bashir asked me, 'Gianiji, tell me, is there God or not?'

I replied, 'I can believe in anything but not God.'

At this Mistri Rahim Bakhsh said, 'I once saw a beautiful girl and started believing in God.'

All this set me thinking. I wondered if I should become part of a popular faith—at least until the Revolution dawns. Islam was attracting me to its fold, and I started feeling that someone who cannot be a Muslim cannot be a communist. In fact, I felt Islam to be closest to the communist ethos. The only difference was that the Muslims were believers in a divine power while the communists were atheists. I thought that I should embrace Islam for the time being but wait for the communist culture to take root. Thus, I would have to be alert because I had to nevertheless retain my atheist's identity. It was a strange thought: that I should be a Muslim and an atheist at the same time. However, I did not share this thought with anyone.

Whenever I ate from the same utensils with the Muslims, I unconsciously felt that I was doing them a favour. They did not even suspect that I could be thinking so. I had not seen any Sikh convert to Islam. On the other hand I had seen Lachhman convert many Muslims to his Nirankari sect.

In solitude, I would start singing my own poems inspired by the news that I would receive about the police encounters in Punjab. The news was coming from those areas where I had once lived in peace. I learnt that an army officer had been killed. The Russian agents were doing all that they had not been able to do earlier. The Chamkaur action had turned the police against us and the killing of the army officer had led to the death of many young men whom the authorities believed were associated with the Naxals. Anyway, whether the Revolution came or not, and irrespective of which party—from the left or the right—ushered it in, the question of culture would always loom large.

———

One evening someone was tuning the transistor and I heard a voice saying, 'Allah . . . hoo . . .' Unable to find any station playing music, he switched off the transistor, slung it over his shoulder and rode away on his bicycle to Mohammadi. All evening I kept hearing the call from the transistor, 'Allah . . . hoo . . .' I paced up and down and I just kept hearing these words.

The next day I asked Bashir to tell me a sentence which I could chant and he told me, 'Allah hoo Akbar.'

I was still an atheist but I asked Bashir the following day, 'How does one become a Muslim?'

Bashir did not lose a moment in enlightening me. He said, 'You just have to recite the Kalma—*La Ilaha Illal La Muhammad Rasoolulla.*' I had heard this before but now I listened carefully and remembered it. After Bashir left, I recited the Kalma and became a Muslim.

I was not happy with the clothes I was wearing and that evening I think I did something amiss at the farm—like tearing my shoes or something like that. The news reached Lachhman. He said, 'Gianiji, I am afraid that you may cause some harm to yourself or to the farm.' He took me along with him to Mohammadi. There he started talking to me and indicated that I was no longer wanted at the farm.

I said, 'It's all right. Give me the fare and I will go to my friend, Musafir.'

He gave me fifteen rupees. I was in a strange state of mind. I went to the market and bought some strange things. These included some colours and a knife. Then I got some potatoes roasted. I already had a few notebooks and magazines in my bag. The five copies of my book *Satluj di Hava* (The Satluj Breeze) had already been given away to friends. I also bought a mirror and a doll to give to Musafir's children. My last purchase was an earthen chillum. Then I got into a bus.

When the bus reached its destination I had two rupees and fifty paise in my pocket. I tore the two-rupee note and threw it outside a urinal. Two blue-turbaned men were travelling by the same bus and one of them was blind. I felt that there was no life left in them. The sweeper at the urinal too could not see anything and sat facing the wall. It was because of this that I tore the two-rupee note and scattered the shreds. I wanted someone to see—to be able to move his eyelids. I wanted everyone to feel and see.

Then I reached the railway station. There were no trains. One train was expected. I started walking along the railway track. I will never forget that night. I sang and danced as I walked. Sometimes I stopped for a while and then spun round and round. A dense forest loomed on both sides of the track but the moon illuminated a path for me. A tall tree in the north was shining in the silvery light. I thought the path was dangerous but something more dangerous was taking place deep within me.

I searched my bag but could not find the chillum. I was despondent at first. But then I felt strengthened by its disappearance. After crossing the woods, I saw a few houses. People were sitting around a bonfire. I joined them and ate my potatoes. I asked them for a piece of jaggery to sweeten my mouth and drank water to my heart's content. I sat there for only a short while so the people did not get a chance to ask me any questions.

I walked some more and passed the Palia station. I was barefoot and once again took the path to the forest. For a while I sat down to rest, but soon I heard the growling of an animal. I gathered some dry grass and leaves and lit a fire. Then I started walking along the railway track in the moonlight. I turned left. I could see the fields and a few people. I looked at my hands and realized that my palms had turned red and yellow with the colours that I had bought and kept in my bag. On my left hand, along the line running across, I saw the shape of the moon around which red, yellow and green colours seemed to have been painted with a brush. Many artists paint the moon round but my hand displayed a crescent moon.

After crossing Palia, I reached the town and the first person I met there was a policeman. I told him straight away that I was going to see Musafir. I was holding my bag, made from an old rug, close to my chest. The policeman pulled out a copy of the *Lakeer* magazine from the bag then put it back. A little further I met a Nepali boy who was digging the ground. He looked at the knife in my hand and wanted to examine it. So I gifted him the knife. In return he gave me twenty-five paise. When I finally reached Musafir's home, he was taken aback at the state I was in. He could not make out what had gone wrong. He just said, '*Allah hi Allah kar piyare.*' (Praise the name of Allah, and Allah alone.)

I stayed one night with Musafir and started off the next day. It was freezing at the railway station. At night the train was empty and I could not see any railway employees. I entered a coach and it was even colder inside. The cold had not troubled me the night before perhaps due to the fire burning inside me; then again, maybe the train was standing in the direction of the cold winds and this was the reason behind the fierce chill. I was in the coach next to the engine. There was a tall and hefty man heaping coals into the engine furnace. I asked him for a piece of coal.

He asked me, 'Where are you going?'

I said, 'Mohammadi.'

He gave me a piece of coal and said, 'Will you reach Mohammadi all by yourself?'

I took out the magazines and notebooks from my bag and lit a fire to keep myself warm. I threw the kurta-pyjama that I was carrying in my bag into the fire. Then I gathered some papers and straws lying on the floor of the coach and lit them. But the fire extinguished soon. I threw the cinders out and, placing my bag on the warm spot, I sat on it. But I was feeling restless and left the coach. I went to a tea shop outside the station. The shopkeeper gave me a glass of tea for one rupee and told me about a truck that would take me further along the way. I boarded the truck.

The truck driver dropped me some distance away, and I started walking again and crossed a cremation ground. I also found a rudraksha bead in a heap of sand. I kept rolling the rudraksha in my hand. I picked up a half-burnt wooden stick. Passing a sugar mill, I had the urge to sweeten my mouth. When I approached the sugar heap, the two boys sitting there screamed and ran inside, scared by my appearance. I put a little sugar in my mouth, ate the leftover potatoes and drank some water.

This path took me back through Purail to the same farm that I had left. I saw Bashir and a few other village boys sitting around a fire. Bashir tore out a piece of paper from his diary and said, 'Go to Mohammadi, this is my home address.'

I started walking towards Mohammadi. It was a night of the full moon and I was wondering how I would accept God. Punjabi littérateur Gurbakhsh Singh had said that there has to be a reason for every action. I put the bead into my pocket but a moment later I was touching my pocket to see if the bead was still there. I was searching my left pocket. When I put my hand inside my right pocket, I found the bead there. I felt Gurbakhsh Singh's words abandon me once and for all; and in that moment I turned into a believer.

I walked on and reached a pond. A man was sleeping by the side of the pond, and a spade was lying by his head. I looked into the pond and saw the silvery net that had been put in the pond. It looked so magical; small, silvery fish were spread out on the net like silver coins. I went to the edge of the pond, pulled out the net and tied it round my head. Passing the sweet shop, I saw a policeman whom I had seen many times before. I told him that I knew Lachhman and Bashir. He patted me on my head and said, 'What a strange state you are in.'

The next day the lambardar took my half-burnt stick and sharpened one end. Now, I had a new, simple weapon. At night I would pierce the stick into the ground and I would hear drumbeats; but when I pulled the stick out, I would hear the sound of a dog howling. I tried this several times; each time the accompanying sounds alternated between the drumbeats and the howling dogs. This was some kind of coded message which was helping me understand my own thoughts.

Earlier I had thought that a cigarette is a cigarette, whether one smokes it at a tea shop or in a friend's home. But when Sayeed gave me a chillum to smoke, the experience was truly spiritual. One day, I saw Sayeed walking with his stick to another village—he looked so much like Ho Chi Minh.

When I met Bashir the following day, he said to me, 'I have a fruit orchard and I want you to live there and take care of it.'

I reached there but my mental state did not change. However, there was no one to question me on the premises. The children would bring me food over there. One day I met the Maulvi Sahib, Naushe Mian, in the town. I touched his knees and said salaam to him. The maulvi said, 'In our faith, touching anyone's feet or knees is forbidden.'

I saw many snake skins in the orchard. One day I also saw a dead snake. First I thought that it was alive and I hit it thrice with a stick; only then was I sure that it was dead. I put it into my lota and placed it on fire. The snake was roasted but it got stuck to the lota and I was not able to clean it. I hit the lota on a brick; it got damaged and had to be replaced. The snake had a little frill at its throat like that of a rooster. It was a black naag (cobra). I had heard that when a naag is killed, the naagin (female cobra) always takes revenge.

That night Bashir took me to his home. I lay down on a cot beneath the banyan tree outside. I was given a hand fan. Some kind of a meeting was going on there. I could hear the man referring to 'skin and bones' many times. I learnt that these men were involved in working with bones and skins of animals but the committee was stopping them from doing this work because the Hindus considered this work low.

The next day I was returning from the orchard after

having my bath. I was wearing just a white lungi and no kurta. Just as I entered the orchard, I saw the naagin disappearing into a hole. It moved very lithely.

There was no one around. I was unable to strike the snake because it was shielded by the branches of the mango trees which nearly touched the ground. I threw my lungi at it, hoping to trap the snake, but it disappeared. I turned to all the snake holes in the orchard and stuffed them with thorny date leaves. One day, I saw the naagin jumping from the grass to the sand and I realized that it had been pierced by a thorn and was in agony. After that, the naagin disappeared forever.

Sometimes Bashir would say things which would ignite my romantic fantasies, like the way he would talk about the henna garden. This was located a little distance away. The garden had rare ketaki plants. It was said that this plant could be grown anywhere but it would blossom only in Mohammadi. The British had tried to experiment by planting it elsewhere but it did not blossom. The ketaki plant has a sharp but pleasant fragrance, something like sweet sharbat. As I was passing through the henna garden, with a basket of mangoes on my head, the ketaki fragrance enveloped me. I put down the basket and looked around. I was told that the ketaki flowers had been plucked. I could see the pale lemon flowers wrapped in banana leaves.

Sometimes girls from Suriya Mohalla along with the daughter of the thanedar would come to the henna garden and chat loudly by the pond. One day the thanedar's daughter, clad in black clothes, was also there, playing with the water coming out of the pipe. The girls were laughing and talking. I was reminded of some very old times.

—◆—

After the mango crop was sold, I came back to the mohalla. There I started learning how to say the namaz. I also got time to read books. I made an effort to learn Arabic. Every morning and evening I would go to the mosque nearby where the maulvi would read Quran Sharif and Hadish Sharif in Arabic and then translate for the benefit of those who did not know the language. By now my mental state had changed for the better. I had cooled down and my restlessness had ended.

I was always against Brahmanvad—the supremacy of the Brahmins—and had started learning namaz while I was still working in the mango orchard. The son of Bashir's partner, a boy called Nawabu, was appearing for his class X examination; he would write down the namaz, bit by bit, and I would learn it by heart. What amazed me was the fact that Nawabu took a lot of interest in this endeavour. He would spend a lot of time teaching me the namaz and also interpreting it for me. How could a boy studying for a final exam spend so much time on such an irrelevant activity? After all, he seemed to have very little to gain from this. One day he told me that even if one did not say the last two stanzas, it was all right and not considered a sin. But if one said them, it was a 'virtue'.

It was then that I realized my folly in calling the activity irrelevant; so far I had never understood the difference between sin and virtue. I had thought that the Revolution was the cure for all ills. I soon learnt to recite the namaz. Initially I was hesitant to learn the religion, fearing that I would be snubbed. But the Muslims considered it a virtue to teach their religion unlike the Hindus who did not do so. Even now many Hindus are so dismissive towards me—or anyone belonging to a lower caste. The other day in Samrala, I was asking a shopkeeper the meaning of some word because he owned a dictionary of Urdu. But the boy's father intervened and told me in plain words, 'Please do not come to the shop for such inquiries.'

The people among whom I was living in Mohammadi were probably Harijans who had converted to Islam. They were very poor but they helped one another a lot. Everyone tried to ensure that no one retired for the night without having eaten something. It was here that I learnt the real meaning of the word jalal (glory). The caste-ridden Hindu society makes even little children prejudiced from the very beginning. But here I saw that the children—even the young girls—would consider it a virtue to give me two daily meals.

Before leaving Punjab I had spent some time with a sadhu who lived in our colony. He had renounced the world when his brother's wife had snatched the roti from his hand. He had tormented his body just like Gautam Buddha had done. Now I was thinking that although he was in search of God, he was not on the right path. He had once told me that when the sadhus would get together, the Chamar sadhus would have to sit separately. I started praying for the sadhu that he should also turn to the path that I had taken so that he would also feel that he was a communist in spite of being a believer. But I could not say the same prayer for my left-wing poet friends and would often fall into a dilemma about what they might be thinking about me. Till recently I had been involved in heated arguments on the merits of being an atheist. I did miss my friends and those fiery arguments. Those were all matters of the head whereas I had completed the journey of the heart by turning to Islam. However, my friends could not understand or appreciate what I had done. I got many letters from old comrades. I answered them to the best of my ability and even wrote in detail of my disturbed days when I had seen the crescent moon appear on my hand. But somewhere deep inside I was upset that my friends like Prem Prakash and others were not able to understand me.

I had heard that without marriage even the greatest of believers are only half-complete. So I was attracted to the idea of getting married and I also thought that it was my duty to do so. Bashir promised that he would find a bride for me. I felt very pleased and visited my home in Samrala with the good news.

When I went to Samrala, I was really happy to meet my family but I wanted to return early so that the police would not start troubling them again. I was thrilled to meet my grandmother. But I could not give her anything since I only had enough money for the return journey. My grandmother believed all that I told her and she too read the Kalma and became a Muslim. My mother and aunt also said they would follow the path that I had taken but they seemed to be in no hurry to convert.

I told my mother that I was to be married and she should arrange some money so that I could go to Malerkotla and get a burqa made for my bride. My mother did not complain about this extortion of three hundred rupees. I took Chacha with me and went to Malerkotla. We went to a mosque. I wanted to inspire Chacha to turn to Islam and I thought that the maulvi would do the needful in this direction. We were given some guavas to eat and word was sent to the tailor to do our work promptly. However, there was not much religious talk. I wanted to get a really beautiful burqa, somewhat like the one worn by a woman standing across the street from the tailor's shop. This was an embellished burqa but the tailor said that making such a burqa would take time. I had to make do with an ordinary burqa.

I learnt that my visit did inspire Chacha to write a letter to the Shiromani Gurdwara Prabandhak Committee, saying that if discriminatory treatment continued with the lower-caste Sikhs then he, along with 300 people, would convert to Islam.

Filled with thoughts of matrimony, I wanted to return quickly to Mohammadi. However, I reached there to find that Bashir had gone back on his word regarding the marriage. He just said, 'We will see.' This was immensely disheartening for me. I was looking forward to the marriage. I had even told everyone back home that the wedding was imminent. So now my letter to them must have been a disappointment because I had to convey that no wedding was going to take place.

In fact, I learnt that many of the folk in Mohammadi wanted to get rid of me because they did not approve of my poetry. This was the centre of the Shariat school and the maulvis were against poetry and thought that the way to hell was paved by writing verses. There was a wide rift between revelation and the creative path of fakiri or mendicancy. It was indeed difficult to bridge the gap.

The qazi of the town was also an indigenous doctor and used to say that God had granted his blessings to medicine so that it cures the sick. But there was the other school which held that no medicine could work without prayer. The qazi had been brought up by his father who was still praised for his wisdom and intellect. It was told that once someone killed a pig and threw it in the Idgah. He went in himself, picked up the dead animal and threw it away. He also called out to the people to calm down and not engage in any violent activity. Sometimes, he would tell a sweeper to go wash his hands and then fetch a paan for him. He would do this to convey to the people that they should follow the religion correctly since the Prophet considered sharing His food with the lepers a matter of pride.

I stayed for three years with Bashir and harvested three crops of mangoes. Not just that, I also worked for a cloth merchant in between. This involved cycling to far-off villages to sell clothes. I also worked as the caretaker of a mill. This mill was a venture of the Islamic Bank, which gave interest-free money against jewellery and other valuables. I worked hard for a living and if I had my own house, I would have saved a considerable amount of money. But I was gaining valuable spiritual knowledge; I had a place to stay in and food to eat; and my mind was at peace. So I was able to take everything in my stride. Even memories of the police torture did not trouble me.

Bashir then sent me to work for a landlord who was now facing poverty. I had some interesting experiences

living with this jagirdar called Bilu Mian. Here I got
a chance to read some books. In one magazine I came
across the ghazal of Faiz Ahmad Faiz: '*Chale bhi aao
ke gulshan ka karobaar chale . . .*' I read it many times. I
came across Syed Mohammad who was a retired Urdu
teacher. He promised to explain the poetry of Iqbal to
me and he also gave me some knowledge about Urdu
words. I was drawn to writing ghazals because I felt
that the phase of blank verse was now a thing of the
past. I started thinking of a Brahmin girl called Lajo in
Samrala. She was a child widow and had spent a lifetime
in penance in the home of her brother. My first couplet
was dedicated to her pain.

A poetry symposium was held in Mohammadi and
I participated in it. Here I came across a dusky girl
reciting beautiful couplets with a lot of emotion. Her
poems made an impact on me. By then I had stopped
working for Bilu Mian and had managed to get the
money he owed me in bits and pieces.

A poet called Asif came to Mohammadi and I got
to know him. He belonged to Bareilly and his father
was a thanedar. He took me to Bareilly to work in his
home. They lived in a proper house and it was shared
by three brothers and their families. There were some
two dozen people living in it including me. Here I
had to work hard day and night in the kitchen. Asif's
mother and sisters-in-law would also be busy in the
kitchen the day the thanedar had to come home. I had

to grind all kinds of spices and help them in preparing different kinds of meat dishes.

I learnt a lot about Urdu pronunciation from Asif when he would come to Bareilly, as he was studying in Rampur. I would also get a chance to meet poets and listen to poetry. However, one day Asif's mother started scolding me and said, 'You won't get any food, I am telling you.'

I told the thanedar that I worked from early morning till midnight and still Amma was telling me that I would not get any food. He replied, 'If Amma curses you, do you think you will get food?'

I started working in the kitchen but my mind was troubled. If Amma's curses had so much power, then what about the power of my own mother's curses? All night I kept thinking that my life was in a mess because of my mother's curses. After a few days, I was scolded once more. It was too difficult for me to bear this and so I returned to Samrala.

POEMS

The Satluj Breeze

When I saw the edges of your veil
wave through the tall rushes
my heart stirred
I saw you in my breath
and in my arms.
The foul breath of the Raj Bhavans
could never touch your pure soul.
You rose from the banks
that held in their sad hearts
the bodies of martyrs
hanged to death
in the Lahore jail—
Here every morning, night
and afternoon is soaked in grief,
songs rise from here
young cattleherds grazing oxen
wade through your waters.
Your flying veils could sail me
to the islands of emotions.
I saw you in the trees
in the sorrow of the wheat fields

in the fragrance of the thorny kikars.
You were always gazing far away
right up to the Kaveri
at the land grabbed away
at the disgraced wheat fields
at the scorched laughter of the paddy fields.
You gaze from far away
at the Raj Bhavans where
hallows of white men still exist.
Your grief became my love
I saw you as my beloved.
Your hands left behind the
enchanted valley of words
and calloused with labour
reached to stroke me
gazing at the moon from the cart.
When the Sun woke up in the morning
in a tangle of ponderous thoughts,
you flashed your fair smile tinged with red
and said, 'Think of me as a flame!'
Even when it gets pitch dark
I will not lose heart.
Your smile, your words
will light up my soul.
Remember that day
when you waters caressed
my shoulders,
and
I felt a gun had been placed there

my eyes were drunk
and the trees seemed to be warriors
galloping away on their horses
with leaves bunched as headgear.
No, I am not sad.
Burma and France quiver.
Slogans echoed by the Indian soil
pierce the walls of the enemy's home
The jungles just have one thing to say:
Forget love! Just watch
the enemy going up in flames.

Evening Tide

Someone has lost all his wages
Another is wiping with his dhoti the
blood off the whip-marks
on weak animals
The evening wears its familiar colours
the footpaths are walking to the basti
the lake is returning from the office
after being shunted out of work
the lake is quenching its thirst for water
the city is walking towards the villages
They are walking away from land
that belongs to another
carrying their straw baskets
The long caravan is moving on
carrying the burden of rebukes
Along the long shadows
children are riding donkeys
Their fathers have dogs in their arms
Pans hang on the backs of their mothers
Babies are sleeping in these pans
The long caravan is moving on

On their shoulders are the bamboos of their shacks
Who are these Aryans, so starved?
Which India's land are they
going to conquer?
The young men love the dogs
Do they not know how to love palaces?
Long starved, they are leaving the
land that belongs to another
The long caravan is moving on
What do they know?
How many are tied to posts
How many burnt alive at the stake
Those who cannot leave the basti
The shadows of the basti trees move on
Someone is holding the legs of tired animals
of tired loves
The long caravan is moving on
The brave tillers of the land walk away
with the burden of shovels on their shoulders
on the wild paths
The love of the fields was murdered last night
Flames rose from the shacks last night
The caravan moves on

Diwali Night

The rushes must be dancing
The waters must be dancing
The waters will stop only to
kiss someone's gaze
Someone's eyes must be
reaching out to the evening
Eyes lit with hope must be
glued to the river bank
O, Autumn Wind!
Take my greetings and say:
'One should never lose heart
thus for anyone's sake'

Flowers of Blood

When one weeps in sleep
and there is no one close
When screams find no words
lips become alien
What does one call those words?
Words that stay awake
all night like a mother . . .

When dew falls down
empty branches look in terror
When leaves stop quivering
in the face of silence
What does one call those words?
Words that walk like sighs
Scared, the birds
start singing all of a sudden

What does one call those words
that stand by you and laugh
Swords searching them rave
for they can't find the flesh

These words are flowers of the blood
that never changes colour
This colour is the same in
every land and every country
When the need arises
the blood is set aflame
Blood-red blossoms bloom . . .

We are very lazy and
darkness shoots like a rocket.

Weeds

I am in love with this flower
with its fragrance of earth
with this little trowel
with its wooden handle
softened by the touch of
many a hand
It is indeed a work of art

This hand in the rains
was a friend to the trowel
Now it looks like a warrior's forehead
with its swollen veins

This warm and stale scent
is rising from these dry weeds
from these withered flowers
from these fading colours
It makes one want to sing
Although the sun rose for them
Pure waters washed them
Winds kissed their faces

But the trowel worked
against the sun
disrespected the winds
scolded the kind waters
So what?
If I the wheat plant
had spread myself
beneath flowing waters
I would also want
the trowel to hit me
Just as the heartless trowel
Pulls out the colours
Of trembling flowers
Is the trowel weeping?
Do not let its tears fall
down on the earth
This girl's neck will double
under the weight

My Country

My country has
another face
Another set
of people
Where a settlement
Half-hungry
Half-asleep
Retires for the night
And counts the stars
To soothe aching limbs

Beyond my country
This is my country
These are my people
Whenever I want to sing a song
To this country of mine
I touch the strings of the sitar
All the sounds from across the seas
Come in accompaniment
Who will welcome them?
Who is filling these rivers
by the boundaries with blood?
My country has another face
Another set of people

Civilization

Who are you?
Why are you hiding your face?
Why do you walk in shadows?
Why are you hiding your nails?
After all, who are you?
Look for the man
who tells fortunes and
wears ancient coins of Rama's age
in his ears
On his body are scars of lashes
Lashes wielded by rulers everywhere
He must know you
Sometimes in the night
he heaves a sigh
endless like the sky
The stars whither
He says:
'The earth is my first love!'
And adds
'I have studded stars in the sky!'

He has trodden over the lands of Jesus
He has walked through the countries of the Buddha
He who wears ancient coins of Rama's age in his ears

Farewell, O Setting Sun

Farewell, O Setting Sun
Do return tomorrow
I will bow before you
but I will not indulge
in the ritual of
offering you water
I will take up arms
Do not return—
People will take up arms
You may even hide the moon
I will take up arms
Don't you know
Humanity is the fire of the sun
whose songs light the lamp
of your glow!
Namaskar!
Farewell . . .
O Setting Sun!

Age and Destiny

Should I tell you your age?
You are as old as an owl
or a mischievous monkey.
Should I tell what's in your fist?
Garbage, lies, deceit!
Should I tell what you want?
Something you will never get.
Should I tell why you sing?
It is your ignorance
that you know all about
earth, destiny of the earth
and age.
What is, what will be,
you are concerned only with your age.

Eunuchs

Eunuchs sing of love
They sing wrong
Eunuchs sing of the tricolour
They sing wrong
They sing of Mona Lisa
or the Greek beauty
They sing wrong
They sing the pain of parting
They sing wrong
They dance and the earth weeps

Just a Thought

Forlorn, I contemplate
a single thought:
that your oiled hair
would bring me salvation . . .

Caste

You love me, do you?
Even though you belong
to another caste.
But do you know,
our elders do not
even cremate their dead
at the same place.

Matter of Faith

How sweet are these words
dedicated to God.
I wish my last words
would be:
'I have complete faith in you!'
I want to steal this line
and dedicate it to the Revolution.

I Am Such a Bitch

Once in a while
that dusky woman
bursts out in happiness
and exclaims:
'I am such a bitch!'

And like me she flings away
much into the flaming ditch
beneath the melting tar
Idols
Books
Her own shoe
The roof under construction
and
Bricks, bricks and more bricks

After Work

After a day's hard work
They tie to the end of
their scarves the daily
wages of their child

They plead for two rotis
They sweet-talk
They talk of their son's mother
They laugh out loud
They grow silent
Then they walk away

Girls Picking Fruit

Naive little girls pick ber
Bare-bodied little girls
gather leaves of the
wild hilly akk plant
bits of broken terracotta
and make rotis of mud
in celebration
of a doll's wedding
They count the dresses
of the dowry
dresses as dirty and old
as their own shirts
They pack the dresses in leaves
The naive little girls pick berries

The girls go out to work
in the fields
Then one day they are married off
Parents bless them with sighs
made of mud rotis and ber
and caress their head

The fragrance of cheap and old clothes
extending to cheap soap and cream
No greater joy comes their way after this
Joy of motherhood
is lost in aches and pains
The mother drinks the blood of life
with a parched roti
Children start walking
they pull her hair
ask her for money
She gives them a few berries
from her pocket with a hard slap
cleaning the vessels
she starts singing of
the love of her husband's
younger brother . . .
Naive mothers joke
as they pick berries
Those who are left alone when
their Lord walks away
on the path of death
lose their youth and struggling
in the mire of life
They neither laugh
nor pick berries

If the inhabitants of other planets
would learn of this
they would turn to stone

and never rise again
If animals were to
experience this
they would run to the forest
screaming in fear of humanity . . .

In Her Father's Fields

Father, sometimes I dance
in your fields
like the soft breeze
I forget
these fields do not
belong to us
We have lost them
and all that we had
Father,
Wild weeds are growing
in your fields
One day the tractors
will dance in your fields

Song to the Satluj

O Satluj Breeze
We will love you always
We come to you once again
Rise and know our hearts
We bring our heads for you
We have braved the seven seas
To quench our thirst for your waters
If your love was to touch a heart
It would turn into the flaming Sun
Every part of us is besieged
The horses gallop down the hills
Corn and millet fields weep
The Black Angrez laughs in glee
O Satluj Breeze

Just like That

Just like that, some storms
Just like that, some tremors
Just like that, some fight
Just like that, some love . . .

Samrala

My town named Samrala
stood for struggle and change
But today it is the terrain
of the drug mafia
Chillums
Poppy husk
Poppy
Opium
Spirit
Heroin
Pills
Smack
Consumers of these
are found lying dead
on the roadsides
and in cremation grounds
Farm dogs feast on their flesh
Science that abuses life
must come to an end

For Us[*]

For us
Trees do not bear fruits
For us
Flowers do not bloom
For us
There is no Spring
For us
There is no Revolution . . .

[*] The first eighteen poems in this selection are taken from the three
anthologies of Dil's poetry, *Satluj di Hava*, *Bahut Saare Suraj* and
Naaglok. The last three poems are excerpts from his long poetic work
published posthumously, *Billa Aj Phir Aaya*.

Afterword

So Long, Samrala

The fragrance of mango blossoms accompanies me as I return from Samrala on an April afternoon, along the road by the harvested wheat fields. Samrala is well known as the birthplace of the famed Urdu writer Saadat Hasan Manto and, of course, my friend Lal Singh Dil. Nearly five years have gone by since Dil passed away and this was my first journey there since the last tributes were paid to him.

The scent of the blossoms is sweet and heady. However, a lingering sadness mingles with the scent as the purpose of this journey itself is so sad: I am attending the last rites of a younger journalist colleague, Kamaljit Rattan. A native of this town, he moved from one highly paid job to another, only to die of a heart attack at the age of forty-nine. In fact, Kamaljit and I struck up a friendship when he read my first article on Dil in the *Indian Express* and came to me to say that he belonged to the poet's town.

Samrala—which Dil said means 'samar-ala' or the

finest fruit—is associated with many memories of painful partings; but it also gave me some cherished moments. Dil's tea shop was a meeting point for local writers and teachers. Some two years ago, Goria, who had been organizing memorial functions for Dil, also died of a sudden heart attack. Goria was born in Manto's Papraudi village, now a part of the town. He would joke, 'Well, I am Manto!' Goria did write some fine stories in Punjabi and both he and Dil were Mantoesque characters drinking from the bowl of death with both hands.

It is heart-wrenching that so many friends from this town went away within a short span of time. Will one remember Samrala as the city of death?

From left to right: Viren Dangwal, Lal Singh Dil, Mangalesh Dabral and Nirupama Dutt

But the strangely illuminated lives of these small-town men—from Manto to Dil, from Goria to Kamaljit—make one think that one will always remember Samrala as a city of life, a city where life was lived against all odds and lived well.

As I stand alone, contemplating this enigmatic city, a gentle breeze laden with the scent of mango blossoms comes to give me solace.

Nirupama Dutt

Appendix

Two Poems on Dil

Roorh the Blacksmith[*]
Amarjit Chandan

Seeing the Urdu alphabet calligraphed
the boy recalls a spindle
The spindle reminds him
of Roorh the Blacksmith
The boy thinks—
Roorh the Blacksmith makes spindles
In the morning prayer at school
He hears thus again—
Roorh the Blacksmith makes spindles
Roorh the Blacksmith makes spindles
To spin yarn
Roorh the Blacksmith makes cloth
Roorh the Blacksmith is straightening
the warped spindle of his life
Roorh the Blacksmith is writing the alphabet.

[*] This poem is inspired by Dil's reaction on seeing the Urdu alphabet
primer for the first time.

Mango Blossoms[*]
Nirupama Dutt

This spring I did not bemoan
the Paradise lost
I awaited mango blossoms
I tasted many times
the delicious juice
that summer would bring
I empathized with conquerors
who came to search for
this fruit in a distant land
Ideally it should have been
the forbidden fruit of paradise
that Eve gave to Adam
This spring I passed
mango groves that scent
the spring air and I did yearn
for the trees lost
forever to the city
I thought of a mango grove
near Samrala town
where I went once
looking for a poet
called Lal Singh Dil

---

[*] This poem about Dil was inspired by a visit to Samrala when I found
   him in a mango orchard along with other writers holding the monthly
   meeting of Samrala Sahitya Sabha as they drank rum.

This spring I liberated
my dead and
celebrated the living
This spring I awaited
mango blossoms and
Paradise was regained

Acknowledgements

I owe much to the poet Amarjit Chandan for being a source of inspiration and for first introducing me to the poetry of Lal Singh Dil. I will remain forever indebted to the magical moments spent with Lal Singh Dil and to his friends, the late Gulzar Mohammad Goria, Hakim Sahib, Baldeep Singh, Sarod Sudeep and the late Pala, for their hospitality towards me in Samrala.

My sincere thanks to my editor at Penguin, R. Sivapriya, for agreeing to publish my translation of Dil's memoirs and poems. Thanks to editors Ambar and Richa for taking the book to its completion.

Gratitude to Chandan, Diwan Manna, Parnab Mukherjee and Swaranjit Salvi for providing pictures of Dil; and to Des Raj Kali, a dear friend Dil and I shared, who was always there to help me out if I was stuck on a word or a phrase.